Lab Manual to Accompany Schneider and Gersting's

An Invitation to Computer Science
Java™ Version

Kenneth Lambert

Thomas Whaley

Department of Computer Science
Washington and Lee University

Brooks/Cole
Thomson Learning™

Australia • Canada • Mexico • Singapore • Spain • United Kingdom • United States

Acquisitions Editor: Kallie Swanson
Editorial Assistant: Grace Fujimoto
Marketing Assistant: Christina De Veto
Advertising: Samantha Cabaluna
Production Coordinator: Stephanie Andersen
Cover Design: Vernon Boes
Print Buyer: Micky Lawler
Printing and Binding: Globus Printing Co.

For more information about this or any other Brooks/Cole product, contact:
BROOKS/COLE
511 Forest Lodge Road
Pacific Grove, CA 93950 USA
www.brookscole.com
1-800-423-0563 (Thomson Learning Academic Resource Center)

For permission to use material from this work, contact us by
Web: www.thomsonrights.com
fax: 1-800-730-2215
phone: 1-800-730-2214

Printed in the United States of America
5   4   3   2

ISBB: 0-534-37489-1

---

www.brookscole.com/compsci/invitation/java

Username: sgjava
Password: lambert

Contents

Preface

This manual and the downloadable software are intended to give students hands-on experience with the fundamental concepts of computer science. Each lab experience assumes that the student has read a chapter in the textbook that introduces and discusses the concepts presented. For example, Lab experiences 5 and 6 on sorting algorithms assume that the student has read Chapter 3 of the textbook.

In cases where there is more than one lab section that covers concepts presented in a chapter of the textbook, the first section should be considered an introduction to the material, while the second section provides more advanced exposure. For example, there are introductory and advanced labs on Java programming, logic circuits, and Turing machines.

Each lab experience begins with a brief discussion of the objectives of the lab experience. Then the student is introduced to the software module that will be used to explore the concepts. Finally, exercises are provided in each lab experience.

The lab manual and software are designed for flexible use:

1. Ideally, students work during a formal lab period with instructor and/or lab assistants available. However, students may also work on their own if no formal lab period is scheduled. Students may work individually or together.

2. Students may do all of the exercises provided in the manual, or the instructor or lab assistant may choose which exercises to require of students, or may add or modify exercises as needed.

3. Most lab work may be turned in either as hard copy or electronically as files.

4. Students may use data files provided with the software, but instructors or lab assistants may add to these files or modify them with the software as needed.

Be sure to keep your original software on the diskettes in a safe place. Please note that the software is for your use only; copying it for the purpose of resale or giving it to others is a violation of federal law (as discussed in Chapter 14 of the text).

Changes to the Revised Edition

The lab software has been completely redone. Its functionality is similar to that of earlier editions, but the look and the feel are "newer." We have added color and made some interfaces easier to use. For example, when a student browses for a file, only files created by the current lab module are visible. Menus have been standardized and commands have been simplified. The software was written in Java and will run on Windows, UNIX, and Macintosh platforms (see installation instructions below). The lab on neural nets had been greatly expanded and enhanced.

Installation Instructions

To download the lab software, go to the Brooks/Cole Web site at

www.brookscole.com/compsci/invitation/java/

There you will see further instructions for downloading the version of the lab software for your particular platform.

Windows and UNIX users will also have to download the Java Runtime Environment (JRE), version 1.2.2 or higher, from Sun at

http://www.javasoft.com/products/jdk/1.2/jre/index.html

or the Java Development Kit (JDK), version 1.2.2 or higher, from Sun at

http://www.javasoft.com/products/jdk/1.2/index.html

The JDK also allows you to compile Java programs. Windows and UNIX users should run the installation program for the JRE or JDK to install Java on their machines. After installing the lab software, these users can double click on the file **Invitation.jar** or enter the command **java -jar Invitation.jar** at the command prompt to launch the lab software. UNIX users may want to change the look and feel to Motif and Windows users may want to change the look and feel to Windows. To do this, press the **Set Look and Feel** button in the main menu. The default look and feel is Metal and is shown in this manual.

Macintosh users will also have to download the Mac OS Runtime for Java (MRJ), version 2.2 or higher, from Apple at

http://www.apple.com/java/

After installing the MRJ and the lab software, these users can double click on the file **Invitation** to launch the lab software.

Acknowledgements

We are grateful to the many reviewers of the new lab software for their helpful comments. In addition, we would like to acknowledge the contributions of several students at Washington and Lee whose work on senior projects contributed to the design of several of the lab software modules: Natasha Edelin, Matthew Hepler, Amber Hinkle, James McCliggott, Graham Powell, and Max Wilson.

The authors also appreciate the extensive feedback from users of the previous editions of the lab manual and software. If you would like to comment on this new edition, or have found an error in the lab manual or software, please send your information to klambert@wlu.edu.

Lab Experience 1

A Glossary and Web Browsing

Welcome to the laboratory. This manual and the accompanying software will provide you with tools to master and enjoy the fundamental concepts of computer science. You should find these tools easy to use. We assume only that you are familiar with the use of a keyboard and a mouse; if you are not, please consult your local authorities (a lab assistant or instructor). Most of the chapters will begin with a set of objectives for the laboratory session. Then there will be a background section giving any information not covered in the text but which is needed for the exercises. Information will also be given on how to use the software module for the particular topic. Finally, there will be a set of exercises.

Objectives

The main objective of this first session is to introduce you to the lab software that you will be using for many of the labs during the course. The module you will use for this laboratory is designed to acquaint you with many of the mechanical skills that you will need as you use the various components of the software package. These skills include rudimentary text processing, the use of menus and buttons, and selections from lists.

A secondary objective is to provide you with a useful organizational tool that you can use to keep up with definitions of important terms as you proceed through the text. In fact, you might want to use this glossary tool for other texts as well. You will be able to organize terms by chapter, add new chapters and terms, and define the terms in any way you like.

In case you have never used a web browser to access the World Wide Web, this chapter provides enough detail to enable you to begin exploring this vast network of information.

Background

The software consists of an application file and a folder containing some example programs. You should run the software by double clicking on the application icon. After closing the sign-on dialog, you should see the menu of buttons as shown in Figure 1.1.

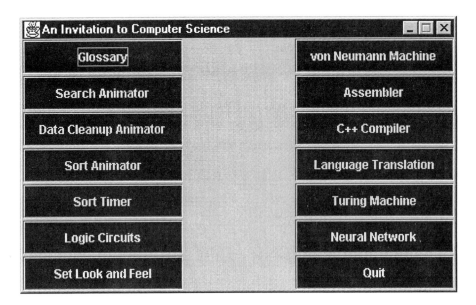

Figure 1.1 The lab software modules

Most of the labs in the course use at least one of the software modules whose names appear in the buttons. These buttons resemble push buttons on real devices such as pocket calculators. You run the function named by the button by clicking once with the mouse on the button. Thus, you open up a software module for the computer science lab with a single click on a button. At this point, UNIX users might want to set the look and feel to Motif and Windows users might want to set the look and feel to Windows. To do this, click the Set Look and Feel button and select the desired look and feel. Or you can keep the Metal look and feel, which is shown in this manual. Now click on the **Glossary** button to open the first lab module.

Window basics

Each lab module opens a window that displays information. The glossary window appears as in Figure 1.2. The window has a title, in this case, **Glossary**, at the top. This window presents you with a view of the different components of a virtual glossary. A printed glossary normally appears at the end of a textbook. It lists important terms and their definitions in alphabetical order. Occasionally, a textbook will have a glossary of important terms at the end of each chapter. An electronic glossary makes browsing for the definitions of terms much easier. Note that our glossary window is divided into smaller parts or panes. Each pane has a label describing the kind of information that appears in it. Right now, the window is opened on an empty glossary, but you can see that there are separate panes for displaying chapter titles, terms within a chapter, and the definition of a term. Our glossary window provides you with a simple tool for creating and maintaining glossaries and for displaying and finding the information in them.

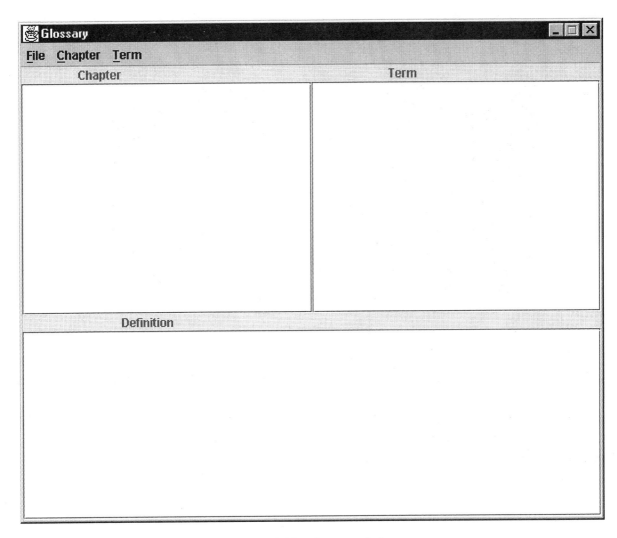

Figure 1.2 The glossary window.

Menu basics

At the top of the window, you will see a menu bar. Along the menu bar are a series of one or more names, like **File**, that refer to pull-down menus. You pull down a menu by holding the mouse button down on the menu's name in the menu bar. Try that for **File** now. The commands under **File** usually are **New**, **Open**, **Save**, **Save as**, and **Quit**.

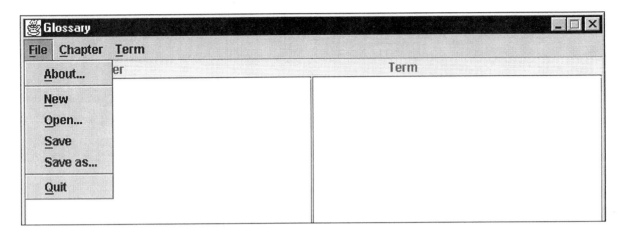

Figure 1.3 The glossary menu bar with File menu selected.

You select a command from a pull-down menu by dragging the mouse to the desired command and releasing the mouse button. **New** creates a new, empty glossary. It will also have the effect of erasing any information from a glossary that happens to be displayed in the window. **Open** allows you to open a file containing a glossary and display it in the window. **Save** allows you to save the glossary displayed in the window to a file. **Save as** allows you to save the glossary to a different file. **Print** lets you print a glossary on a lab printer. **Quit** appears in every **File** menu and allows you to exit the application.

Opening files

Your software comes with a file that contains a glossary for the first two chapters of the textbook. Select **Open** from the **File** menu. You will be presented with a file dialog that allows you to browse for and select a file to open. The initial file dialog for each lab software module connects to a folder named **Examples** and shows just those files that can be opened for the module (Figure 1.4).

Figure 1.4 A file dialog with a glossary file selected.

The names of files containing glossaries, if there are any, will appear in a list. Your options at this point are to open the selected file, select a different file to open, move to a different folder or disk drive to browse for files, or cancel the operation altogether. For now, open the sample file called **example.glo** by clicking the **Open** button or pressing the Enter key. If all goes well, you should see the contents of the sample glossary in the glossary window.

Browsing for information

Initially, only the chapter titles are displayed in the **Chapter** pane. View the terms defined for the first chapter by clicking on its title. You should see a list of terms in the **Term** pane. You can switch to the terms for another chapter by selecting that chapter with the mouse. Try that for the second chapter now, and watch the changes in the **Term** pane. To view the definition of a given term, select any term in the **Term** pane. You should see the definition in the **Definition** pane. Once again, you can switch to the definition of any other term by selecting the term in the **Term** pane. You can also make more terms visible by scrolling through the **Term** pane.

An electronic glossary makes browsing easy and natural. Rather than turning pages of a book to find the end of the desired chapter, and then turning more pages to find the desired term, you click the mouse a couple of times to find a definition of a term in a chapter. In fact, our glossary is just a particular application of a simple electronic database that could serve just as well to organize information according to some other hierarchical scheme of classification.

Searching for information by query

Another way to find the definition of a term is to click the option **Find** that appears in the **Term** menu. You will be prompted for the name of the term whose definition you desire to look up:

Figure 1.5 Running a query for a term.

You type the term at the keyboard, and click **OK** or hit the carriage return to start the search. Alternatively, you can click **Cancel** to back out of a query. If the system cannot find the term anywhere in the glossary, it will inform you with a message dialog:

Figure 1.6 A failed query.

When you click **OK** in the message dialog, you will be allowed to continue working with the glossary. If the term is found, however, the panes in the window will be refreshed so that the chapter and target term are selected and the definition of the term is displayed. Try a query for a term that you know is in the glossary now.

Editing a glossary

The glossary application allows you to edit an existing glossary or build one up from scratch. The application behaves like a word processor with respect to files. The information that you edit in the window is just a working copy of the permanent glossary in a file. If you want to make your changes permanent, you should pick **Save** from the **File** menu. If you want to back out of the changes you have made, you can pick **Open** from the **File** menu to recover an existing glossary or **New** from the **File** menu to start over.

Let's start a new glossary. Select **New** from the **File** menu to clear the window. Then pull down the **Chapters** menu. As shown in Figure 1.7, you will see two choices, of which only **Add** is active:

Figure 1.7 Adding a chapter to the glossary.

When you select **Add**, the system prompts you for the title of a chapter to be added to the glossary:

Figure 1.8 Entering the title of a chapter.

If you click **OK**, the window will display the chapter title (such as Chapter 1) you entered in the **Chapter** pane. Now pull down the **Terms** menu. Note that only **Add** seems to be active in this menu. **Delete** is not active because no term has been selected for deletion.

Figure 1.9 Adding a term to the glossary.

This is an example of a user-friendly interface: the system provides cues on the screen that tell you what you're allowed to do with the data that is available.

Now you are ready to add a term to the first chapter. Pick **Add** from the **Terms** menu. You will be prompted for a new term. Type in **computer science**, and click **OK**. Your window should look like this:

Figure 1.10 The glossary after adding a term.

To enter the definition of this term, start typing in the definition. If you don't remember the definition, you can type in a reasonable definition since this part is just for practice anyway. As you type, you will see your words in the **Definition** pane. When you have finished entering the definition, it would probably be a good idea to save your glossary in a file. Select **Save** from the **File** menu and enter a new name (like **mygloss.glo**).

Editing text within text panes

After you have entered the definitions of terms in a glossary, you can return to edit them whenever you like. The pane of the window in which a definition appears is called a text pane. The standard shortcut keys for editing commands are associated with any text pane. For example, on a Windows platform, these commands are Ctrl-x, Ctrl-c, and Ctrl-v for **Cut**, **Copy**, and **Paste**, respectively. These commands assume that you have selected an area of text and wish to manipulate the area with the command. You select text in a text pane by clicking the mouse at the beginning of the area, and holding the mouse button down while dragging the mouse to the end of the area. It may take a couple of tries to get the technique of selection right. When you succeed, the desired chunk should appear in inverse video (white letters on a black background). *Deletion* the simplest (and most dangerous) command. It deletes the text from the pane, and you will not be able to recover the deleted text (except by reopening a permanent file). An easy way to delete a selected area of text is to hit the **delete** or **backspace** key on the keyboard. The other three commands utilize a temporary area of computer memory called a *buffer* for saving the selected chunk of text, so that you can restore it to the pane if you wish. **Cut** removes the selected chunk from the pane, and saves it in the buffer. **Copy** saves the selected area in the buffer, but does not remove it from the pane. When you wish the selected area in the buffer to be restored to the pane, you click the mouse at the desired position in the pane and press the shortcut key for **Paste**. Go ahead and try all of these commands now on some sample text.

Introductory web navigation

In Chapter 12 of the text you will learn a great deal about networks, the Internet, and the World Wide Web. For our purposes now, we can view the "web" as a large number of **hypertext** documents, called **pages**, which are stored on computers around the world and are generally accessible to the public. A page may contain text, graphics, video, and sound as well as **links** to other locations within the page or to other pages on the web. A link is a highlighted item of text or an icon that can be clicked to move to another web location. Each page has its own address, called a Uniform Resource Locator or URL. Associated with a link is the URL of the target location.

Among the many types of software available for working with the web are **web browsers** that enable you to navigate the web by specifying URLs and following links, **search engines** that search the web for specified topics, and **web editors** for creating and editing web pages. In order to access the web, you will need to make use of one of the web browsers. Two popular browsers at the time of writing of this manual are Netscape's Navigator and Microsoft's Network Explorer. Either of these has the basic features that you will need for doing the web exercises of this manual. Figure 1.11 shows the main menu bar for Netscape's Navigator. Modern web browsers have many capabilities other than simply navigating the web. These include managing email, downloading documents and software from other computers to your computer, and participating in user groups with people of common interests. Here we shall focus on the most basic operations of web navigation. If you have not used a web browser, you will need to become familiar with the browser on the system you are using. As you work with the browser more, you will learn more of the advanced features from classmates, lab assistants, the extensive online help systems included with the browsers, and by just trying new things on your own.

Figure 1.11 A web browser.

A user of a browser can set a specific web page to be his or her **home page**. This is the page that is accessed when the browser is first started. The home page may be a page that the individual has created with his or her personal information or it may be the main page of the school or company that owns the computer system being used. This page serves as a "home base" for the user. You can always return to your home page by clicking on the **Home** button. Once you have a web page on your screen, you can read the page just like any other computer document; i.e. you read the page on the screen and use scroll devices as needed. However, if you encounter a highlighted object on the page, chances are this is a link to another page. You can tell whether or not the item is a link by moving the cursor over the item. If it is a link, the cursor will change to a particular shape, say a hand with pointing finger, to indicate a link at the spot. If you click on the link, the browser will attempt to locate the page using the associated URL. This may simply move to another location on the same computer or possibly to a page on a computer half way around the world. If the browser is successful, the target page will appear on your screen. The time it takes to obtain the page depends on several factors such as the traffic on the network at the time, the network distance of the target machine, the speed of the network connections used for the retrieval, and the size of the page. You will find that pages with lots of images take much longer to access You will have a good understanding of why this is true once you have studied Chapter 12 of the text. Unsuccessful attempts by the browser to locate a page may be due to the fact that the computer with the target page is not available at the time, the URL for the page has been changed, or the author of the page has removed the page. As you navigate through the web, the browser keeps a history of the URL's that you have visited. At times you may want to reverse your steps for a few pages. You do this by clicking on the **Back** button. Each time you click the Back button you move to the immediately preceding page in your journey. If you wish to move to a page which you accessed many steps earlier, pull down the **Go** menu. There you will find a list of many of pages that you have accessed. If you know the URL of a page you would like to visit, you simply type the URL into the **Location** field and hit Enter on the keyboard. You will learn more about URLs in Chapter 12 of the text. For now, just type the URLs exactly as given. Another feature provided by the browsers is the ability to maintain a list of **bookmarks**. If you find a page that you know you will want to visit on future occasions, rather than keep up with the URL yourself, you can pull down the **Bookmark** menu and select **Add Bookmark**. The browser will then add the URL of the current page to its list of bookmark URLs. If you ever wish to go to such a page, you simply pull down the Bookmark menu and select the page you would like to access.

Exercise 1.1. Adding terms to a glossary

Open the glossary that came with the lab software. Click on "Chapter 1: An Introduction to Computer Science" in the Chapters pane. This should bring up the list of terms for Chapter 1 of the text. One term that is missing from Chapter 1 is "unambiguous operation". Choose **Add** from the **Terms** menu and enter this term. Type in the definition for this term:

> An operation that can be understood and carried out directly
> without needing to be further simplified or explained.
> (Section 1.3.1)

Now select "Chapter 2: Algorithm Discovery and Design" and add the term "infinite loop" with the following definition:

> A loop in which the termination condition is never met, thus
> resulting in the loop body being executed forever or until
> the algorithm is aborted by external intervention. (Section 2.2.3)

Choose **Save** from the **File** menu to make sure your additions are stored permanently.

Exercise 1.2 Adding a new chapter

Choose **Add** from the **Chapters** menu and add a "Chapter 3: The Efficiency of Algorithms". Now proceed to add the following two terms for Chapter 3:

> efficiency - An algorithm's careful use of resources such as space
> and time. (Section 3.2)

> benchmarking - Comparative timings used to rate one machine
> against another with respect to one specific algorithm, or
> for rating how sensitive a particular algorithm is with
> respect to variations in input on one particular machine.
> (Section 3.2).

Now choose **Save** from the **File** menu to make sure your additions are stored permanently.

Exercise 1.3.   Making changes to a definition

Select Chapter 1 from the Chapters pane. Then select the term "algorithm" from the term pane. Here you should find four definitions: a dictionary definition, an informal definition, a formal definition, and a bad pun definition. The first three of these are from the text, but the fourth has no place in our glossary. Use the technique discussed earlier to select the text for this fourth definition. Once you have the text selected, hit the **delete** key on your keyboard. Again, be sure to save your changes as before.

Exercise 1.4.   Using the Find button

Select **Find** from the **Term** menu and search for the term "pseudocode". The term should be found and selected from the terms of Chapter 2. Copy the definition into the appropriate place in the Worksheet page for this lab. Now search for the term "unambiguous operation". If things go well, the definition you added earlier should be retrieved. Finally, try finding the term "assembly language". As you see, this term is not covered in the Chapters we have in the glossary so far.

Exercise 1.5.   Turning in your work

If you have network access, turn in your glossary file from the previous exercises to your instructor (instructions for doing this will vary from school to school; so your instructor will have to show you how to do this). Now under the **File** menu, select **Quit**. This should return you to the main Lab Software window. There you should click on the **Quit** button.

Exercise 1.6.   The web browser and your home page

Follow your local instructions to start up your web browser. Click on the **Home** button to be sure you have your home page active. Look in the **Location** field to find the URL of your home page. Copy this URL into the appropriate place on the Worksheet.

Exercise 1.7.   Accessing a page by URL

Now you should practice accessing a page by entering a URL. For example, type the URL www.wlu.edu/~compsci into the location field of the browser (refer back to Figure 1.11). When you hit the Enter key, you should see the page of the Computer Science Department at one of America's leading small colleges.

Exercise 1.8.   Accessing a page by following a link

Now click on the link "Majoring in CS". This should bring up a page with course requirements for a typical computer science major. Copy the URL for this page onto the Worksheet.

Exercise 1.9.   Using the Back button and adding a Bookmark

Now return to the previous page for the web exercises by clicking on the **Back** button of the browser. Since you might want to visit this page often, it is probably a good idea to add this as a bookmark. To do this, choose **Add Bookmark** from the **Bookmark** menu.

Exercise 1.10.   Home again

Now return to your home page by clicking on the **Home** button of the browser.

Worksheet
Lab Experience 1
A Glossary and Web Browsing

Name: _____

Course: _____

Exercise 1.4.   Using the Find button

    Pseudocode:

Exercise 1.6.   The web browser and your home page

    URL of your home page:

Exercise 1.8.   Accessing a page by following a link

    URL of web exercise page for this lab:

Lab Experience 2

Search for a Value

Objectives

This laboratory experience will introduce you to the use of a simple algorithm animator for the sequential search algorithm that is covered in Section 2.3.1 of the text. By observing the data movement as the algorithm is being executed, you should be able to gain a greater understanding of what the algorithm does and how it does it. Once this goal is achieved, you will use the animator to obtain some empirical data concerning the number of steps required for finding various target values. Using this data, you will be asked to draw conclusions that anticipate the kind of study you will encounter in Chapter 3 where we turn our attention to the efficiency of algorithms.

Background

To begin the lab experience, click the **Search Animator** button on your lab software menu (Figure 2.1):

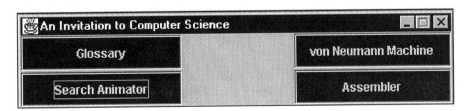

Figure 2.1 Choosing the Search Animator.

At this point, a new window will appear (Figure 2.2). Note the following components:

- An **Algorithm** menu. This menu lets you select the algorithm to run (either search for a given value or search for the maximum value).
- The text of the current algorithm (search for a given value when the window is opened).
- A set of three command buttons (**Run, Step,** and **Reset**).

- A graphic image of an array of values and a box waiting to be filled with the user's target value.
- A slider bar to control the running speed.

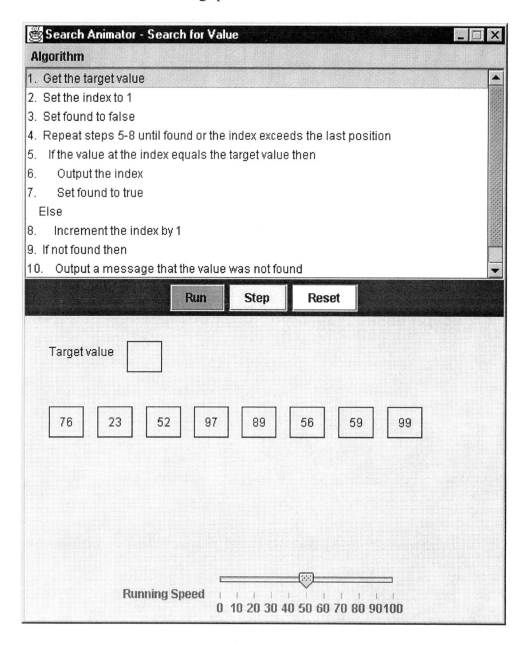

Figure 2.2 The Search Animator.

For purposes of this animation, we chose to search through a list of numerical data rather than a list of names. Before each run of the algorithm, you can click on the **Reset** button, and a new set of data will be generated. Notice that the first step of the algorithm is shaded. As the execution progresses, the next step to be executed will be shaded. This will enable you to keep track of exactly where the algorithm is in its execution and correlate what is happening to the data on the screen with the step of algorithm being executed. You will also notice that the pseudocode differs slightly from what is given in the textbook. This was done to correspond with the visual cues given in the animation. Remember that pseudocode is not intended to be rigid and exact, but rather to provide the constructs needed to convey in a fairly precise way how the algorithm performs its task:

When the animator executes the input statement, you will see a ***prompter box*** asking you to enter the target value. You should enter the value for which the algorithm should search. Typically, you will enter one of the data values in the list; but if you wish, you may enter a value not in the list to observe what happens in this case. When you enter the target value, you type in the number and then hit the **Enter** key or click on the **OK** button in the prompter box. When an output statement is executed, the output message will appear in a ***message box***. This box will stay on the screen until you hit the **Enter** key or click on the **OK** button.

If you click on the **Run** button, the animator executes the entire algorithm, pausing only for input and output. Clicking on the **Step** button causes just a single step of the algorithm to be executed or pauses execution during a run. Clicking the **Run** button during stepping resumes execution as a run. Given our goals of gaining insight into the nature of the algorithm and gathering empirical data, you will primarily use the step mode of operation.

In the lower right corner of the animator is a slider bar that adjusts the speed at which the animator runs. By sliding the bar up (faster) or down (slower), you can select a speed that is appropriate for you. It is possible to change from one speed to the another during the animation of the algorithm.

Exercise 2.1.   Resetting the data

Click on the **Reset** button a few times and observe what happens to the data set. Explain what seems to be happening on the Worksheet.

Exercise 2.2.   Running the animation

Move the slider bar at the bottom of the window to the right to decrease the running speed or to the left to increase it. Click on the **Run** button. Enter as the target value the last value in the data list. As the animation runs, the steps may be executed at a speed that makes the details hard to follow. However, by watching the shaded statement change, you should be able to observe the primary looping nature of the algorithm. Click on the **Reset** button and try this again.

Exercise 2.3.   Stepping with the animator

Reset and try out the step mode by clicking on the **Step** button. Enter a value from the middle of the data list and continue stepping by repeatedly using the **Step** button until the stop statement has been executed.

Exercise 2.4.   Location of target and number of steps

In this exercise, choose the first element in the list as the target and step through the algorithm. As you step, keep a careful tally of exactly how many times each step is executed. Enter this data into the first row of the table on the Worksheet. Compute the total number of steps executed and enter this into the table.

Now reset the animator, use the second data element as the target, and enter the results into the second row of the table. Continue to do this until a distinct pattern becomes apparent. At this point, use the pattern you observe to complete the first eight rows of the table. In the last row of the table, assume that the target is the kth data element and express your entries in terms of k. For example, entries might be k or k+1, etc. Do not fill in the entry in the Total column for the last row.

Exercise 2.5.   Formula for the pattern

In this exercise, you will derive a formula that will give the number of steps required by the search algorithm in terms of the position of the target. To do this, simply add the entries in the bottom row of the table from Exercise 2.4 and use algebra to simplify the expression obtained. Give your formula on the Worksheet.

Exercise 2.6.   Prediction for larger data set

Based on the pattern observed in Exercise 2.5, how many steps would you expect it to take to find the 100th element, if there were that many in the list? Give your answer on the Worksheet.

Exercise 2.7.   Average number of comparisons

As you will see in Chapter 3, one measure of work done by an algorithm is the number of comparisons of elements that the algorithm must perform. In the Search for Value algorithm, the comparisons are made in Step 5. Under the assumption that the target is as likely to be in any one position in the list as in any other position, the best way to measure the number of comparisons is to average the number of comparisons required for the various positions of the target. Compute the average number of times Step 5 must be executed for the eight-element list by averaging the numbers in the first eight rows of the Step 5 column of the table in Exercise 2.4. If the list only had seven elements, we would average the first seven of the numbers in this column. Try computing this average for a few values for the list size. Give a formula for the average number of comparisons if there are n elements in the list.

Worksheet
Lab Experience 2
Search for a Value

Name: _____

Course: _____

Exercise 2.1.   Resetting the data

What happens when you click on the reset button?

Exercise 2.4. Location of target and number of steps

Target Step	Step 1	Step 2	Step 3	Step 4	Step 5	Step 6	Step 7	Step 8	Step 9	Step 10	Total
Element 1											
Element 2											
Element 3											
Element 4											
Element 5											
Element 6											
Element 7											
Element 8											
Element k											

Exercise 2.5.   Formula for the pattern

Exercise 2.6.   Prediction for larger data set

Exercise 2.7.   Average number of comparisons

Average for 8-element list:

Average for 7-element list:

Average for 4-element list:

Average for 2-element list:

Average for n-element list:

Lab Experience 3

Search for the Largest Value

Objectives

This laboratory experience will continue in the spirit of Lab Experience 2. This time you will use an animator for the search for largest value algorithm, covered in Section 2.3.2 of the text. The primary goal is to enhance your understanding of exactly how the algorithm works by seeing what the algorithm does as you step through its execution. Again you will be asked to gather some empirical data and to try to make conjectures based on the results.

Background

As in Lab Experience 2, you begin the lab experience by clicking on the **Search Animator** button on your lab software menu. This time, after the search animator window opens, you should select the **Search for Largest** option under the **Algorithm** menu.

In the exercises you will be asked a couple of questions that require the knowledge of two facts from probability. First, if we have n numbers chosen at random (as we get when we click **Reset**), there are

$$n! = n(n-1)(n-2)\cdots(2)(1)$$

different possible orderings of the numbers. For example, with the 8 items in the animator, there would be $8\cdot7\cdot6\cdot5\cdot4\cdot3\cdot2\cdot1 = 40,320$ different orders in which we could list the 8 elements. The idea is that there are n elements from which to choose the first element. Having chosen the first element, there are n-1 elements left from which to choose the second element. Thus there are n(n-1) ways in which to choose the first two numbers in the list. Continuing in this way leads to the formula above.

The second fact has to do with the likelihood that a given item will occur in a given location. The point here is that a given item, in terms of relative size, is as likely to occur in one position as another. So, if there are n items, the probability that a particular one of the items shows up in a specific position would be 1/n. For example, the probability that the second largest item would show up in position 6 when we click **Reset** would be 1/8 with the animator having 8 items. This means that if you reset many, many times, you should see the second largest show up in this position about 1/8 of the time. This would require many trials in order to see this fact play out.

Exercise 3.1.   Stepping

Use the **Step** button to execute the algorithm two or three times until you understand exactly how the algorithm works and how the animation corresponds to the steps in the pseudocode window. Remember to click the **Reset** button when you are ready to start over with a new set of data.

Exercise 3.2.   How many positions does the location marker achieve?

Observe that with the 8 pieces of data, there are always 7 passes through the loop (n-1 if there were n pieces of data). However, the number of positions that the location marker takes on (Step 7) depends on the relative order of the data. You will now make use of the animator to explore this dependence in more depth. Using the step mode, you should now gather data from 10 executions of the algorithm and enter the results on the Worksheet. For each data set, you should copy down the entire data set and keep up with the position of the location marker L and the data value at position L each time L moves. For example, if the data set were 20,15,25,30,42,18,72,11, then you would copy the entire list as the data set. The original position of L would be position 1 and the value in that position is 20. Therefore, you would enter 1 for the location and 20 for the value. When the L marker moves, list the location that it moves to and the value there. Continue until the algorithm terminates. Once you are sure of how this works, it is fine to just click the **Reset** button and copy the relevant data down without stepping through the entire execution (just be sure that you know what will happen).

Exercise 3.3.   Determining the values at the Location marker by scanning

Look at the data obtained in Exercise 2. Notice that the values stored in the positions taken on by the Location marker form a *subsequence* of the original data set; i.e., the values are taken from the original set in the same relative order as in the original set. On the Worksheet, explain in your own words how to scan the list from left to right and pick out the values that will be in this subsequence.

Exercise 3.4.   Fewest positions for the L marker

What would be the smallest number of positions that Location could possibly take on? Describe the special conditions under which this would happen. Approximately, how often would you expect this to occur? Put your answers on the Worksheet.

Exercise 3.5.   Largest number of positions for the Location marker

What would be the largest number of positions that Location could possibly take on? Describe the conditions under which this would happen. Approximately, how often would you expect this to occur? Put your answers on the Worksheet.

Exercise 3.6.   Likelihood of many positions for the L marker

How would you compare the likelihood that Location would take on three different values with the likelihood that Location would take on seven different values? Would you expect the likelihood that Location takes on three different values to be much smaller, about the same, or much larger than the likelihood that it would take on seven different values? Answer on the Worksheet.

Worksheet
Lab Experience 3
Search for Largest Value

Name: _____

Course: _____

Exercise 3.2.   How many positions does the location marker achieve?

Data Set 1:   Data Set 6:
Location :   Location :
Value   :   Value   :

Data Set 2:   Data Set 7:
Location :   Location :
Value   :   Value   :

Data Set 3:   Data Set 8:
Location :   Location :
Value   :   Value   :

Data Set 4:   Data Set 9:
Location :   Location :
Value   :   Value   :

Data Set 5:   Data Set 10:
Location :   Location :
Value   :   Value   :

Exercise 3.3.   Determining the values at the Location marker by scanning

Explanation for finding subsequence:

Exercise 3.4.   Fewest positions for the L marker

Fewest positions for Location: _____

Special conditions for this to occur:

How frequently would this occur?

Exercise 3.5. Largest number of positions for the Location marker

> Largest number of positions for Location: _____

> Special conditions for this to occur:

> How frequently would this occur?

Exercise 3.6. Likelihood of many positions for the Location marker

Lab Experience 4

Data Cleanup

Objectives

This laboratory experience will serve to reinforce your understanding of the shuffle-left algorithm (Section 3.3.1 of the text) and the converging pointers algorithm (Section 3.3.3 of the text). You will use simple animators much like those of the previous two lab experiences. Once you fully understand the operation of these algorithms, you will gather data to assist in making connections between the number of "copy" operations performed and the number and positions of the bad data items in the original data sets.

Background

To begin the lab experience, click the **Cleanup Animator** button on your lab software menu. Under the **Algorithm** menu, there are options for the **Shuffle-Left** algorithm and the **Converging Pointers** algorithm. Be sure to select the one that applies to the exercise you are currently doing.

For the Shuffle-Left algorithm, the number of times a data item is copied to another position depends not only on the number of bad data items (0's), but also on the positions in which the bad data are located. As you will see, the number of copy operations generated by a given bad data item depends on the position in which the data item is located when it is detected by the if-statement (Step 5 in the animator pseudocode) and on the number of items in the entire list. The position where a bad data item will be detected can be determined by the position of the item in the entire list and by its position in the list of bad data (is it the first bad item, second bad item, etc.). Once these relationships are understood, it is possible to determine the total number of copy operations required, knowing only the original positions of the bad data items. You will explore this connection in the exercises.

For the Converging Pointers algorithm, you will find that the situation is dramatically different as far as the number of copy operations is concerned.

Exercise 4.1.   Running the Shuffle-Left animation

Select the **Shuffle-Left** algorithm from the **Algorithms** menu. Use the **Run** button and observe the "loop inside a loop" nature of this algorithm by watching the animation. The general idea is that the L marker moves to the right trying to detect 0's. Each time it detects a 0, the R marker moves to the right shuffling the data items to the left. Try this three or four times, remembering to use the **Reset** button to prepare for each run.

Exercise 4.2.   Stepping with the Shuffle-Left animation

Now use the **Step** button to walk through the algorithm on a couple of data sets. This allows you to see the fine details of how the algorithm works. Once you are comfortable with this, move on to Exercise 4.3.

Exercise 4.3.   Copy operations and positions of 0's

Now we will explore the question of the number of copy operations needed to do the data cleanup with this algorithm. This time click the **Reset** button until you get a data set with three or four 0's. Record the location of the 0's in the original data set on the Worksheet. Now step through the algorithm, carefully observing and recording where each 0 is located when it is detected by the if-statement of Step 5. Also, observe and record how many copy operations (Step 10) are executed as the given 0 is "squeezed out".

Exercise 4.4.   Drawing conclusions

In this exercise, you are asked to draw conclusions based upon your observations in Exercise 4.3. It may be that you will need to repeat Exercise 4.3 a time or two before you see the relationships. Record your answers on the Worksheet.

With an 8-element list, if a 0 is detected in position k, how many copy operations are needed to squeeze it out?
Suppose there were n items in the list rather than 8?
If the first 0 is originally in position k, where will it be when it is detected by the if-statement?
If the second 0 is originally in position k, where will it be when it is detected?
If the third 0 is originally in position k, where will it be when it is detected?
If the jth 0 is originally in position k, where will it be when it is detected?
If the first 0 is originally in position k, how many copy operations will it generate?
If the third 0 is originally in position k, how many copy operations will it generate?

Exercise 4.5.   Using the conclusions

Using the conclusions you formulated in Exercise 4.4, suppose we have 200 items in the original list with three 0's located in positions 47, 110 and 162. Tell exactly how many copy operations would be performed by the Shuffle-Left algorithm in cleaning up this data set (Worksheet).

Exercise 4.6.   Running and stepping with Converging Pointers

Now choose the **Converging-Pointers** algorithm from the **Algorithms** menu. As before you should work with the run and step modes until you have a clear picture of how the algorithm works.

Exercise 4.7.   Copy operations with Converging Pointers

Using the step mode, explore the question of the number of copy operations in terms of the number and location of the 0's for this algorithm. For each trial run, write down the data set on scratch paper and keep up with the number of copy operations. Try to find a data set where the number of copy operations is the same as the number 0's, record the original data set on the Worksheet. Try to find a data set where the number of copy operations is different from the number of 0's and record this data set. As a **challenge problem**, formulate a clear description of data sets where the number of copy operations is different from the number of 0's.

Exercise 4.8. Converging Pointers with larger data sets

Answer Exercise 4.5 using the Converging-Pointers algorithm instead of the Shuffle-Left algorithm.

Exercise 4.9. Markers and good data items

When the animator completes its run, how can we tell where the good data items are located in terms of the markers?

Worksheet
Lab Experience 4
Data Cleanup

Name: _____

Course: _____

Exercise 4.3.   Copy operations and positions of 0's

Original position of first 0:
Position where first 0 is detected:
Number of copy operations generated by first 0:

Original position of second 0:
Position where second 0 is detected:
Number of copy operations generated by second 0:

Original position of third 0:
Position where third 0 is detected:
Number of copy operations generated by third 0:

Exercise 4.4.   Drawing conclusions

Number of copy operations generated by 0 detected in position k of 8-element list:

Number of copy operations generated by 0 detected in position k of n-element list:

Position where first 0 is detected if it is originally in position k:

Position where second 0 is detected if it is originally in position k:

Position where third 0 is detected if it is originally in position k:

Position where jth 0 is detected if it is originally in position k:

Number of copy operations generated by first 0 in n-element list if it is originally in position k:

Number of copy operations generated by third 0 in n-element list if it is originally in position k:

Exercise 4.5.   Using the conclusions

Number of copy operations for 200-element list with 0's in positions 47, 110 and 162.

Exercise 4.7.   Copy operations with Converging Pointers

Data set where number of copy operations is same as number of 0's:

Data set where number of copy operations is different from number of 0's:

Challenge - when will number of copy operations differ from number of 0's?

Exercise 4.8.   Converging Pointers with larger data sets

Number of copy operations for 200-element list with 0's in positions 47, 110 and 162.

Exercise 4.9.   Markers and good data items

Where are the good items in terms of the markers?

Lab Experience 5

Sort Animations

Objectives

In this laboratory session, you will once again make use of a simple animation program to get more feeling for the way algorithms work. This time you will be working with the selection sort algorithm (Section 3.5.2 of the text) and two other well-known algorithms for sorting, the bubble sort algorithm (Exercises 14-16 of Chapter 3 of the text) and the quick sort algorithm which is discussed in the background section. The first objective is to learn how the algorithms work. The second objective is to gain some understanding of the amount of work done by the algorithms by measuring the number of comparisons made or the number of exchanges made. In the next lab experience, you will make use of a very different kind of animator to test the theoretical results obtained by classifying the algorithms in terms of the comparisons made.

Background

One of the most common tasks of computer programs is the sorting of numerical or character data. This is due to the enormous number of reports that must be produced with the data in a specified order and the enormous number of searches for specified records. As soon as you have compared the efficiency of binary search of ordered data with sequential search of unordered data, you will appreciate the importance of maintaining data in ordered structures in large database systems.

The importance of sorting accounts for the large amount of work that computer scientists have devoted to designing and analyzing various algorithms for sorting data. It may seem that one algorithm would become the "standard" sorting algorithm which everyone would use. This is not the case, however, and most computer programmers have a small collection of such algorithms that they can readily implement or already have implemented. The reason for this is that there are several factors that determine the appropriateness of a specific algorithm. For example, the simple algorithms tend to work well on small sets of data, say 50 or fewer items, but become too slow to be useful on larger sets. Some algorithms work well for data that is somewhat ordered to begin with, while other algorithms do their worst on data already ordered. Some of the least efficient algorithms are popular simply because they are easy to understand and therefore easy to implement by beginning programmers.

The software module for this lab is accessed by clicking on the **Sort Animator** button of the main button menu of the lab software. The various sort algorithms appear as options under the **Sort Algorithm** menu. The selection sort algorithm has been covered thoroughly in the text. Notice that the version here is "expanded," in the sense that the individual steps of the search for largest algorithm of Chapter 2 are included here rather than given as a single step. At the lowest level all of these steps must be carried out. Of course we do not include the steps for obtaining the data since we do not get new data each time the algorithm finds the largest element of the unsorted section. The bubble sort algorithm is comparable algorithm that is introduced in the exercises at the end of Chapter 3 of the text. The insertion sort algorithm is another

31

"simple" sort algorithm that will not be covered in detail here unless your lab instructor chooses to introduce it. You are certainly encouraged to explore this algorithm on your own. The basic idea is that moving from the left, each element is "inserted" into its proper sorted position among the elements preceding it in the list.

The selection, bubble, and insertion sort algorithms all have the feature that they make many passes through the data, essentially placing one data item per pass. The effect of this is that these algorithms fall into the same general class in terms of efficiency. To obtain an algorithm that will be fundamentally better requires an entirely different approach. There are sort algorithms which, like the binary search algorithm, are based on the "divide and conquer" strategy for problem solving. For sorting with this strategy, the basic plan is to gain efficiency by sorting pieces of the list and then having some way to put the sorted pieces back together into a sorted whole. The quick sort algorithm is one such algorithm.

The general plan for quick sort is to first partition the elements of the list with the smaller elements going into the first section and the larger elements going into the second section. Once the two sections are themselves sorted, it follows that the entire list will be sorted. The pseudocode for this basic version is

1. Partition list with small elements in first part, large elements in second part.
2. Sort the first part.
3. Sort the second part.
4. Stop.

To implement this plan, we must settle two obvious questions. First, how do we accomplish the partitioning of the list, and second, how do the sections get sorted?

Let's deal with the second question first. To sort a sublist, we use the same strategy as on the entire list; i.e., we partition the sublist and sort the remaining sublists. An algorithm like this which makes use of itself to solve smaller subproblems of the same type is called a *recursive algorithm*. Binary search is sometimes presented as a recursive algorithm. Clearly, this process of partitioning and applying the sort algorithm to smaller lists must not go on forever. At which point we stop subdividing is somewhat a matter of choice. For our purposes, we will stop if the sublist to be sorted has no more than two elements. If it has only one element, there is nothing more to do, and if it has two elements, we simply compare the elements and exchange them if they are out of order. With this level of refinement, the pseudocode looks like

1. If the list to sort has more than 1 element then
2.   If the list has exactly two elements then
3.   If the two elements are out of order then
4.   Exchange them
5.   Otherwise
6.   Partition list with small elements in first part,
         large elements in second part
7.   Apply Quick Sort to the first part
8.   Apply Quick Sort to the second part
9. Stop.

The strategy for the partitioning is to choose an element from the list to serve as a "pivot" element. Then we compare the other elements with the pivot element, putting the elements less than or equal to the pivot into the first section and putting the elements larger than the pivot into the second section. This leads to two more questions - how to choose the pivot and how to get each element into the appropriate section of the list. The ideal pivot element would be the median of the list. This would lead to an even split which in turn leads to the most efficient sorting. However, it is important that the choice of the pivot element be made quickly; so, it is not feasible to look for the median each time. Some versions of quick sort simply take the first element, others take the median of the first, last and some middle item, and so on. For the purposes of our animator, we chose to consider the first three elements of the sublist and take the median value of these as the pivot.

Once the pivot element has been chosen, we exchange it with the first element in the sublist. The partitioning algorithm that we use employs two markers, a lower marker (L) that starts at the second element and an upper marker (U) that starts on the last element of the sublist. Now we keep moving L to the right until we come to an element larger than the pivot (everything to the left of L belongs in the first section). Next we move U to the left until we come to an element smaller than the pivot (elements to the right of U are in the second section). If L and U have not crossed, then the element at L belongs in the second section, and the element at U belongs in the first section; so we exchange them. We continue this process of moving L to the right, moving U to the left, and exchanging until the markers cross. At this point, U should be on the last element of the first section. We then exchange the pivot element with the element at U. The elements to the left of U (the pivot) comprise the first section and the elements to the right of U comprise the second section. The following is the pseudocode for the version that is used in the animator:

1. If the list to sort has more than 1 element then
2.   If the list has exactly two elements then
3.   If the two elements are out of order then
4.   Exchange them
5.   Otherwise
6.   Exchange the median of the first three elements with the first
7.   Set the pivot marker (P) on the first of the elements
8.   Set the lower marker (L) on the second element
9.   Set the upper marker (U) on the last element
10.   Repeat steps 11-16 until L is to the right of U
11.   While the element at L is less than or equal to the element at P do step 12
12.   Move L to the right one position
13.   While the element at U is larger than the element at P do step 14
14.   Move U to the left one position
15.   If L is left of U then
16.   Exchange the elements at L and U
17.   Exchange the elements at P and U
18.   Apply Quick Sort to the sublist of elements to the left of U
19.   Apply Quick Sort to the sublist of elements to the right of U
20. Stop

If you have trouble following this discussion, remember that the purpose of the animator is to help you understand the details of the algorithms. Once you have worked with the animator, matching steps in the pseudocode with the actions in the animation, come back and read these paragraphs again.

Exercise 5.1. Stepping with Selection Sort

Choose the **Selection Sort** algorithm from the **Sort Algorithm** menu. Click on the **Step** button until you see exactly how the algorithm works. Each time, before clicking, try to anticipate what is going to happen when you click on the button.

Exercise 5.2. Show what would happen with Selection Sort

Suppose the original data set consists of the numbers

34 52 21 14 67 59 30 18

Show on the Worksheet the exact arrangement of the data after 3 major passes have been made by the Selection Sort algorithm, where a major pass is completed each time we come back to Step 2.

Exercise 5.3.   Counting exchanges and comparisons with selection sort

Click on the **Reset** button and write down on the Worksheet the data set that is generated. Now repeatedly click the **Step** button until the animator completes its task of sorting the data. As you do this, keep track (Worksheet) of how many exchanges are made (Step 9), and also keep track of how many comparisons (Step 6) are made. Do this for each pass and then get the two totals for the entire sorting.

Exercise 5.4.   Compare with the theory for selection sort

How does the total for the number of comparisons obtained in Exercise 5.3 compare with the formula of $(1/2)n^2 - (1/2)n$ given in the text (note that n=8 for the animator)?

How many comparisons would it take for n=20? How many exchanges? Record your answers on the Worksheet.

Exercise 5.5.   Stepping with bubble sort

Choose the **Bubble Sort** algorithm from the **Sort Algorithm** menu. Click on the **Step** button until you see exactly how this algorithm works.

Exercise 5.6.   Show what would happen with bubble sort

Suppose the original data set consists of the numbers

$$34 \quad 52 \quad 21 \quad 14 \quad 67 \quad 59 \quad 30 \quad 18$$

Show on the Worksheet the exact arrangement of the data after 3 major passes have been made by the bubble sort algorithm where a major pass is completed each time we come back to Step 2.

Exercise 5.7.   Counting exchanges and comparisons with bubble sort

Click on the **Reset** button and write down on the Worksheet the data set that is generated. Now repeatedly click the **Step** button until the animator completes its task of sorting the data. As you do this, keep track of how many exchanges are made (Step 6), and also keep track of how many comparisons (Step 5) are made. Do this for each pass and then get the two totals for the entire sorting.

Exercise 5.8.   Compare with selection sort

How do the totals for bubble sort (Exercise 5.8) compare with those of selection sort (Exercise 5.3)? How many comparisons would you estimate for bubble sort with n=20? Can we say exactly how many exchanges there will be with n=20? Record your answers on the Worksheet.

Exercise 5.9.   Stepping with quick sort

Choose the **Quick Sort** algorithm from the **Sort Algorithm** menu. Click on the **Step** button until you see exactly how this algorithm works. Notice that each time the algorithm starts to sort one of its sublists, a begin marker (B) and an end marker (E) mark the beginning and end of the current sublist. Also notice that executing the stop command simply indicates the ending of the work on the current sublist. Be sure you understand the details before moving on.

Exercise 5.10. Show what would happen with quick sort

Suppose the original data set consists of the numbers

34 52 21 14 67 59 30 18

Show on the Worksheet the exact arrangement of the data after the data has been partitioned the first time (when we come to Step 18 the first time).

Exercise 5.11. Counting exchanges and comparisons with quick sort

Click on the **Reset** button and write down on the Worksheet the data set that is generated. Now repeatedly click the **Step** button until the animator completes its task of sorting the data. As you do this, keep track of how many exchanges are made (Steps 4, 6, 16 and 17), and also keep track of how many comparisons of data elements (Steps 11 and 13) are made.

Exercise 5.12. Binary search

(Binary search is covered in Section 3.5.3 of the text. If you have not yet studied binary search, then you may want to return to this exercise later.) Click on the **Reset** button to obtain new data in the array. Then pick **Binary Search** from the **Sort** menu. What happens? Why? Notice that each time through the loop, the number at the C marker is compared with the target number. This happens once each time C takes on a new value. Therefore, we can count the comparisons by counting the number of positions that C takes on. Using step mode, first choose the first element in the list as the target and record the number of positions that C takes on. Now do this choosing the second element in the list as the target and continue for each element in the list. Give the largest number of comparisons made for any target in the list. Give the average number of comparisons. What would be the largest number of these step needed to find a target if we had 16 data items rather than 8? How about 32 data items? How about 1024 data items? Record your answers on the Worksheet.

Worksheet
Lab Experience 5
Sort Animations

Name: _____

Course: _____

Exercise 5.2. Show what would happen with selection sort

Original data set: 34 52 21 14 67 59 30 18

After 3 passes:

Exercise 5.3. Counting exchanges and comparisons with selection sort

Original data set:

Pass	Exchanges	Comparisons
1		
2		
3		
4		
5		
6		
7		

Totals

Exercise 5.4. Compare with the theory for selection sort

Compute the value of $(1/2)n^2 - (1/2)n$ with n=8:

How does this compare with the number of comparisons found in Exercise 5.3?

Number of comparisons for n=20:

Number of exchanges for n=20:

Exercise 5.6.   Show what would happen with bubble sort

Original data set: 34 52 21 14 67 59 30 18

After 3 passes:

Exercise 5.7.   Counting exchanges and comparisons with bubble sort

Original data set:

Pass	Exchanges	Comparisons
1		
2		
3		
4		
5		
6		
7		

Totals

Exercise 5.8.   Compare with selection sort

Compare the number of exchanges for bubble sort with selection sort:

Compare the number of comparisons for bubble sort with selection sort:

Number of comparisons with bubble sort for n=20:

Any comments about the number of exchanges with bubble sort:

Exercise 5.10.   Show what would happen with quick sort

Original data set: 34 52 21 14 67 59 30 18

After first partitioning:

Exercise 5.11.   Counting exchanges and comparisons with quick sort

Original data set:

Make tally mark for each exchange:

Total exchanges:

Make tally mark for each comparison:

Total comparisons:

Exercise 5.12. Binary search

What happens when you first try to choose Binary Search?

Why should this happen?

Number of comparisons with first number as target:

Number of comparisons with second number as target:

Number of comparisons with third number as target:

Number of comparisons with fourth number as target:

Number of comparisons with fifth number as target:

Number of comparisons with sixth number as target:

Number of comparisons with seventh number as target:

Number of comparisons with eighth number as target:

Largest number of comparisons:

Least number of comparisons:

Average number of comparisons:

Largest number of comparisons if n=16:

Largest number of comparisons if n=1024:

Lab Experience 6

Sort Timing

Objectives

In this laboratory session, you will be introduced to a new way to view a sort algorithm in action. Here you will view the data graphically as the algorithm progresses. This gives interesting and informative information about the nature of the algorithm and about the intermediate arrangements of the data. Also, the software used in this session will allow you to time various sort algorithms on different sizes of data sets. In this way you will be able to test some of the theoretical results obtained by analyzing the efficiency of the algorithms mathematically.

Background

First, let's discuss how the data being sorted can be viewed graphically as the sort algorithm is executing. The best way to understand this approach is to consider the list of data as a function. Suppose we have the list of numbers 5, 7, 2, 8, 3. Now this list can be viewed as a function, say L, where L(1)=5, L(2)=7, L(3)=2, L(4)=8, and L(5)=3. We can now draw the scatter plot graph of this function as in Figure 6.1. It is interesting and insightful to watch the scatter plot as the list is being sorted. As you will see, the structure of the data at intermediate steps differs significantly depending upon the algorithm being used. Of course these graphs will not show the steps in the detail of the animator in the previous lab, but they will show the structure of the data in a more useful way. As an example, let's carry through the selection sort algorithm as it works on the data in the list above. The first change that we observe is when the largest element, 8, is exchanged with the last element, 3.

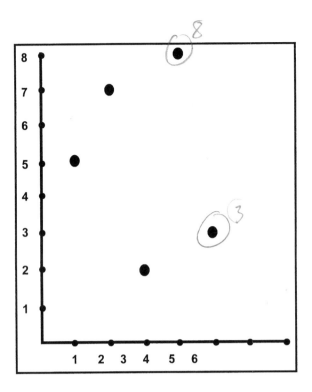

Figure 6.1 Scatter Plot Graph of a List.

After this exchange, we have L(4)=3 and L(5)=8, and the other function values are as before. The resulting scatter plot is shown in Figure 6.2.

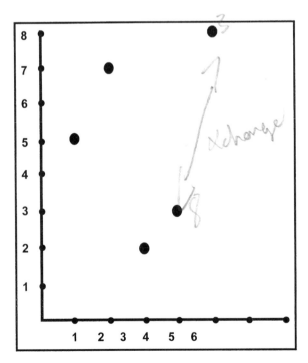

Figure 6.2 Graph After First Exchange.

The graphs after the subsequent exchanges are shown in Figures 6.3 and 6.4. Even with this tiny data set, you should be able to see clearly the sorted and unsorted sections after each step. The software we use in this lab allows us to watch the scatter plots for several sort algorithms. You will be asked to observe the scatter plots and answer questions relating the patterns formed with the particular algorithm under study.

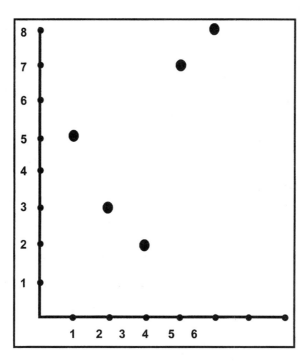

Figure 6.3 Graph After Second Exchange.

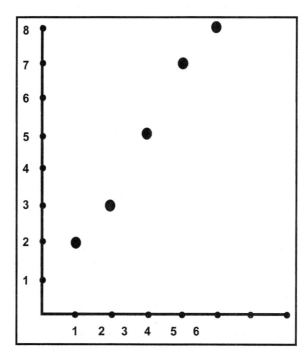

Figure 6.4 Graph After Third Exchange.

The second goal of this laboratory session has to do with timing sort algorithms to see how well the theoretical efficiency classifications hold up in practice. You will be asked to time a given algorithm for a relatively small data set and then, based on the efficiency classification of the sort algorithm, you will make a prediction as to how long that algorithm would take to sort a larger size data set. Then you can do actual runs of the algorithm to see how good your prediction is.

It is important to keep in mind that the classifications are rather crude. For example, we have lopped off all terms except for the dominating term. So, these classifications are useful only to give "ball park" estimates or to understand the general growth rate for the algorithm. You should also keep in mind that the performance of most of these algorithms depends on the data to be sorted. We've seen this already when using the sort animator, and by viewing the scatter plots for multiple runs of the same algorithm this will become even more apparent. Also, we should mention that the times being recorded are not fair tests for the algorithms if all that is needed is for the numerical data to be sorted. Here we are timing not only the sorting, but also the graphing of the scatter plots. In general, the graphing is orders of magnitude slower than the internal sorting. As you'll see throughout your study of computer science, manipulations that take place in the memory of the computer are much faster than manipulations with external devices such as printers or monitors.

For the timing exercises, you need to be familiar with the classifications of the algorithms. You recall that selection sort, as analyzed in Section 3.5.2 of the text, is a $\theta(n^2)$ algorithm. A similar analysis of the bubble sort algorithm (see Exercises 14-16 from Chapter 3 of the text and Lab Experience 5) shows that it is also $\theta(n^2)$ as is the insertion sort algorithm.

A complete analysis of the quick sort algorithm is beyond the level of this course, but can be found in most texts on computer algorithms. To get some idea of how this algorithm provides an improvement over the other algorithms considered so far, we'll do a very rough analysis for the idealized situation where we get nearly even splits for all of our partitions. To carry out a partitioning with a list of k elements requires that each element other than the pivot be compared with the pivot, thus k-1 comparisons are required. Depending on how we choose the pivot, another comparison or two may be required. To keep the algebra simple, let's say k comparisons are needed. If we begin with an n element list, then we'll have n comparisons to partition it into two sublists each containing approximately n/2 elements. These sublists will eventually be partitioned, requiring n/2 comparisons each, thus n more comparisons. These partitionings result in four more sublists each of size approximately n/4. Partitioning these requires about n/4 each or another n total. Remember that we stop when we get sublists of size 1 or 2. At each "level" we're requiring about n comparisons. But how many levels will there be? We're asking "How many times must we divide n by two before the result is 1 or 2?" The answer is approximately Lg n. Thus the total number of comparisons in this idealized situation is approximately Lg n times n, or n Lg n. It turns out that the average case analysis also leads to the conclusion that quick sort is a $\theta(n \text{ Lg } n)$ algorithm. One way to think about this is that instead of n^2, we have one of the n's replaced with Lg n, a fundamental improvement.

As an example of how we might use the Big Oh classifications to make predictions, suppose we run a sort on a list of size 1000 using selection sort, and suppose it takes 1 second to complete the sort. Let's use this information to obtain a rough approximation of how long it would take the same algorithm on the same computer to sort a list of size 100,000. Since selection sort is dominated by an n^2 term, we can use the formula $T(n) \cong K n^2$ where $T(n)$ is the time to sort n elements, K is some constant, and $\cong$ indicates approximation. Now K can be approximated using the given information:

$$T(1000) \cong K\ 1000^2,\ \text{or}$$
$$1 \cong K\ 1000^2,\ \text{and}$$
$$K \cong 1/(1000^2)$$

It follows that

$$T(100,000) \cong K\ (100,000)^2$$
$$\cong (1/1000^2)(100,000)^2$$
$$= 100^2\ \text{seconds}$$
$$\cong 2.8\ \text{hours}.$$

On the other hand, if the first sorting had been done with quick sort (with the same result), we would use $T(n) \cong K\ n\ Lg\ n$, and our approximation would proceed as follows:

$$T(1000) \cong K\ 1000\ Lg(1000)\ \text{or}$$
$$1 \cong K\ 1000\ Lg(1000),\ \text{and}$$
$$K \cong 1/(1000\ Lg(1000))$$
$$\cong 1/(1000\ 10)$$
$$\cong 1/(10,000)$$

It follows that

$$T(100,000) \cong K\ 100,000\ Lg(100,000)$$
$$\cong (1/10,000)(100,000\ Lg(100,000))$$
$$\cong (1/10,000)(100,000\ 16.6)$$
$$\cong 166\ \text{seconds}$$
$$\cong 2.8\ \text{minutes}.$$

This hypothetical example serves to show the dramatic difference between $\theta(n^2)$ and $\theta(n\ Lg\ n)$ as the size of the data set increases.

You should now run the lab software package and click the **Sort Timer** button. You should now see a screen like the one in Figure 6.5. The **Algorithm** menu provides a choice of sort algorithms including the ones discussed so far together with some other well-known algorithms. The **Points** menu gives a choice as to the number of points to be sorted. The time it takes to do the sort is shown in the lower right. The **Reset** button stops execution and generates a new set of data. The **Run** button executes the chosen sort algorithm on the data set. The **Pause** button temporarily stops the execution so that we can study the scatter plot. Clicking **Pause** again or on **Run** resumes execution of the algorithm.

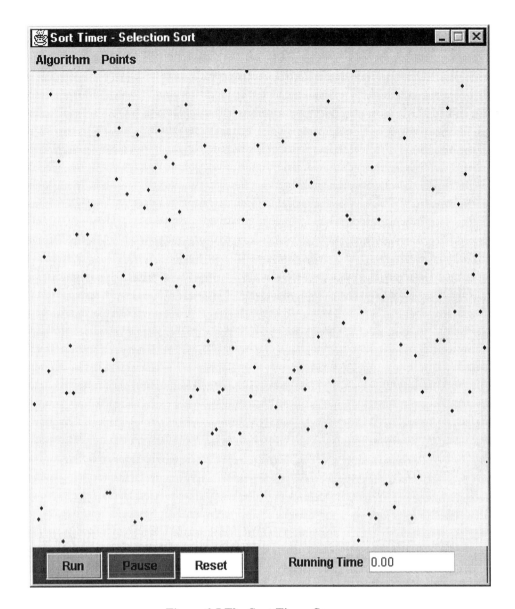

Figure 6.5 The Sort Timer Screen.

Exercise 6.1. Running selection sort

The selection sort algorithm is the current algorithm when the simulator starts up. From the **Points** menu, experiment with various numbers of points. Each time click on the **Run** button and watch the scatter plot until the sort completes. Notice the sorted and unsorted sections during the run.

Exercise 6.2. Where were the sorted points originally?

Now choose enough points that you will be able to stop pause the sort during the execution. Click on the **Reset** button to get a new set of data. Click on the **Run** button again, but this time click on the **Pause** button when the sorted section contains about half of the points. The scatter plot should look something like that in Figure 6.6. The following series of questions are based on this diagram. Before answering, think carefully about the details of the selection sort algorithm. Record your answers on the Worksheet.

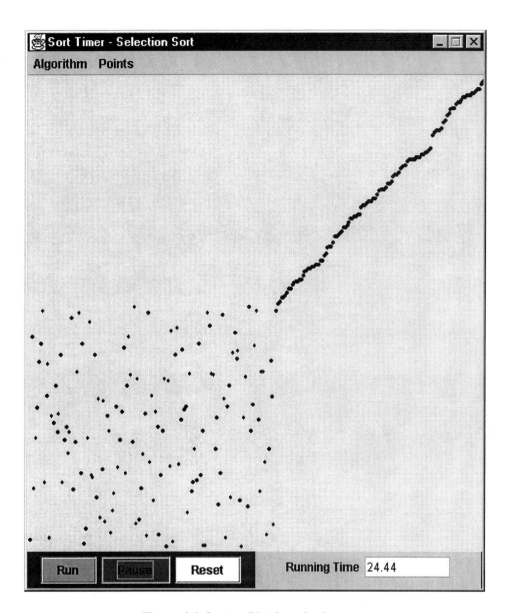

Figure 6.6 Scatter Plot for selection sort.

The sorted part now shows up roughly in the upper right quadrant of the graph. Is it possible that any of these sorted points may have originated in the lower half of the graph before being "moved"? Explain your answer.

Exercise 6.3.   Where were the unsorted points originally?

Is it possible that any of the points in the lower left quadrant were originally in the lower right quadrant? Explain your answer.

Exercise 6.4.   Direction of motion

Let L mean that a point has moved to the left, and R mean that a point has moved to the right; so, LR would mean that the point has moved to the left and later moved to the right. Which of the pairs LL, LR, RL, RR are possible and which are impossible? Explain.

Exercise 6.5.   Running bubble sort

Now choose the bubble sort algorithm from the **Algorithm** menu, and click on the **Reset** button. Proceed as before to watch a run or two of the algorithms. As before, on one of the runs, pause when the sorted section contains about half of the points (Figure 6.7). The next series of questions refer to this figure. Give your answers on the Worksheet.

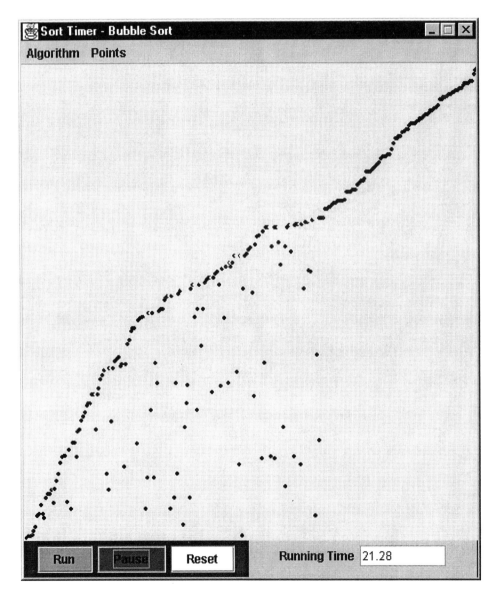

Figure 6.7 Scatter Plot for bubble sort.

Exercise 6.6.   Where did the lower right points go?

Which part of the graph now contains the points that were originally in the lower right section of the graph? Explain your answer.

Exercise 6.7.   Some moved, but aren't sorted

Some points have moved to the right, but are not yet in the sorted section. Can you tell where they are located?

Exercise 6.8.   Contrasting Selection and Bubble

Discuss differences you note between the scatter plots for selection sort and bubble sort. Explain these differences in terms of the algorithms. In other words, if you were given a scatter plot of a partially completed sort, how could you tell whether it was selection sort or bubble sort?

Exercise 6.9.   Direction of motion

Which of the pairs LL, LR, RL, RR are possible and which are impossible with bubble sort? Explain.

Exercise 6.10.   Running quick sort

Now choose the **Quick Sort** algorithm from the **Algorithm** menu and do a few runs with different numbers of points. Notice the patterns that are formed. Also, notice approximately how long the runs take. Choose a number of points that will allow you to pause during the run. Now do a run and pause at approximately one fourth of the time for completion; if the entire run takes about 16 seconds, then pause at about 4 seconds. You should have a graph something like that in Figure 6.8. Notice the "boxes" of points arranged diagonally from lower left to upper right. Your graph may have a different number of boxes and may have a different sized line formed at the left. The next series of questions will refer to this figure. Give your answers on the Worksheet.

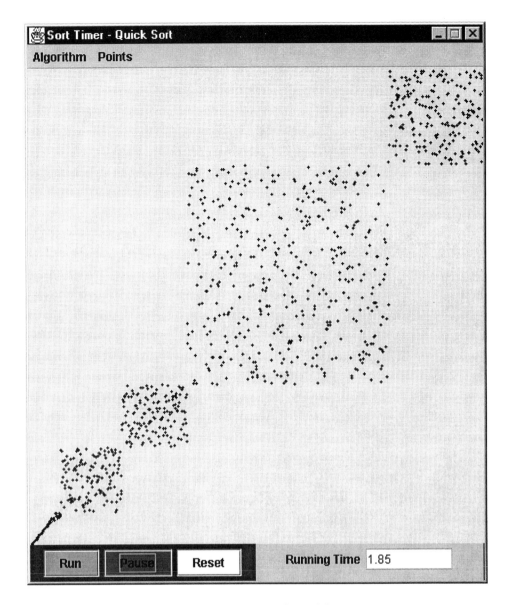

Figure 6.8 Scatter Plot for quick sort.

Exercise 6.11. Pattern formed by quick sort

How many "boxes" of points do you seem to be in the figure? Indicate the box that you think the algorithm is sorting. Indicate the box that you think will be sorted next.

Exercise 6.12. Timing bubble sort

Choose the **Bubble Sort** algorithm from the **Algorithm** menu and experiment with the number of points to find the smallest number of points that will require at least 5 seconds to sort. Let N indicate this number of points. Now do three or four runs with N points and record the times. Compute the average time and use the average and the fact that bubble sort is $\theta(n^2)$ to predict how long it will take to sort twice this number of points (2N points). Always show your work. For a short cut, if an algorithm is $\theta(n^2)$, then doubling the size of the data set should multiply the time by 4. Now do a couple of runs with 2N points to test your prediction. How well did the predictions work out? Compare this with the naive conjecture that doubling the data set would double the work to be done. Keep in mind that our estimates are only rough predictions. Record your answers on the Worksheet.

Exercise 6.13.   Timing insertion sort

Repeat Exercise 6.12 only using insertion sort instead of bubble sort. Insertion sort is also $\theta(n^2)$.

Exercise 6.14.   Timing quick sort

Choose the **Quick Sort** algorithm from the **Algorithm** menu and experiment to find the least number of points that will require at least 3 seconds to sort. Let N represent this number of points. Now do three or four runs with N points and record the times. Compute the average and use the average and the fact that quick sort is $\theta(n \text{ Lg } n)$ to predict how long it will take to sort 2N points and 4N points. Now test your predictions by doing actual runs. How well did this work out? Use the Worksheet for your answers.

Exercise 6.15.   A Mystery Sort

There are two sort algorithms, merge sort and heap sort, under the **Algorithm** menu that we have not studied. Choose one of these algorithms and find the least number of points that requires at least 3 seconds to sort. Let N represent this number of points. Now do three runs with N points and record the times. Compute the average and make a prediction for the time for 2N points assuming first that the algorithm is $\theta(n^2)$. Then make a prediction for 2N points assuming that the algorithm is $\theta(n \text{ Lg } n)$. Now do a couple of runs with 2N points and record the times. Based on the results of this experiment, do you think the algorithm is probably $\theta(n^2)$ or $\theta(n \text{ Lg } n)$? Use the Worksheet for your answers.

Exercise 6.16.   Timing selection sort

Choose the **Selection Sort** algorithm from the **Algorithm** menu and experiment to find the least number of points that will require at least 3 seconds to sort. Let N represent this number of points. Now do three or four runs with N points and record the times. Compute the average and use the average and the fact that selection sort is $\theta(n^2)$ to predict how long it will take to sort 2N points. Now test your predictions by doing actual runs. How well did this work out? If your results were anything like ours, then your results were not all that good. We'll explore this matter further in the next exercise. Use the Worksheet for your answers.

Worksheet
Lab Experience 6
Sort Timing

Name: _____

Course: _____

Exercise 6.2.   Where were the sorted points originally?

Could any of the sorted points have originated in the lower half of the graph?

Explain why or why not:

Exercise 6.3.   Where were the unsorted points originally?

Could any of the points in the lower left quadrant have originated in the lower right?

Explain why or why not:

Exercise 6.4.   Direction of motion

Is LL possible (could a point move left and then move left again)?

Explain why or why not:

Is LR possible?

Explain:

Is RL possible?

Explain:

Is RR possible?

Explain:

Exercise 6.6.   Where did the lower right points go?

Where are the points that were originally in the lower right?

Explain:

Exercise 6.7.   Some moved, but aren't sorted

Some points have moved to the right, but are not yet in the sorted section. On the graph below, draw a line around the set of points that you think fit this description.

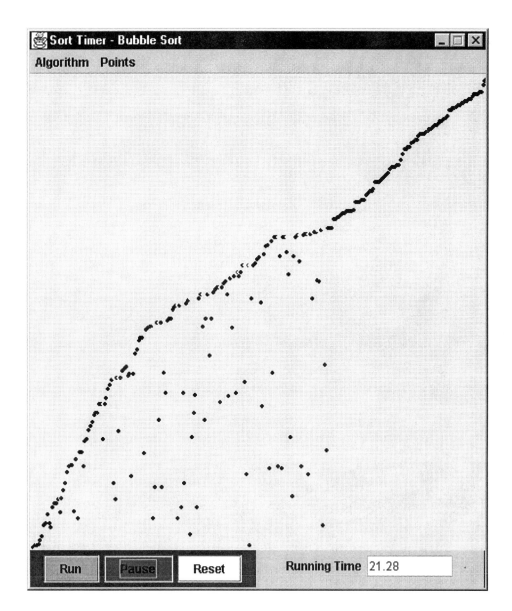

Exercise 6.8.   Contrasting Selection and Bubble

Describe a difference between a selection sort scatter plot and a bubble sort scatter plot:

Explain this difference in terms of the steps the algorithms perform:

Exercise 6.9.   Direction of motion

Is LL possible for bubble sort?

Explain why or why not:

Is LR possible?

Explain:

Is RL possible?

Explain:

Is RR possible?

Explain:

Exercise 6.11.   Pattern formed by quick sort

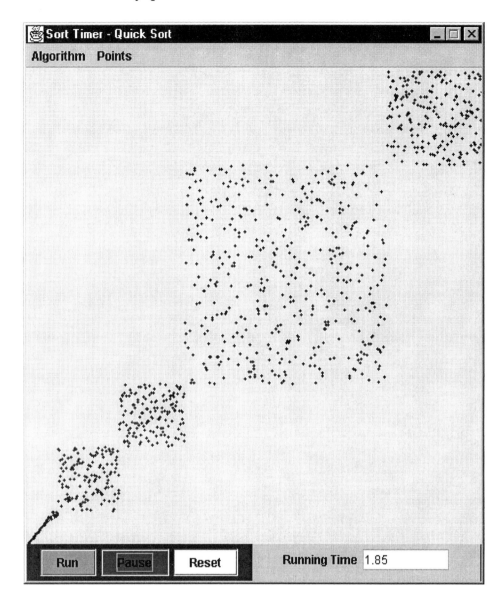

How many "boxes" of points do there seem to be in the figure?

Indicate the box that you think the algorithm is sorting by putting the number 1 above the box.

Indicate the box that you think will be sorted next by putting the number 2 above the box.

Exercise 6.12.   Timing bubble sort

Smallest number of points that requires 5 seconds (N points):

Give times for 3 runs with N points:

Average time:

Estimate of time for 2N points (show computations):

Give times for 2 runs with 2N points:

Do you think the theoretical estimate was fairly accurate or not?

How well would doubling the time for N points work as a prediction for 2N points?

Exercise 6.13.   Timing insertion sort

Smallest number of points that requires 5 seconds (N points):

Give times for 3 runs with N points:

Average time:

Estimate of time for 2N points:

Give times for 2 runs with 2N points:

Do you think the theoretical estimate was fairly accurate or not?

How well would doubling the time for N points work as a prediction for 2N points?

Exercise 6.14.   Timing quick sort

Smallest number of points that requires 3 seconds (N points):

Give times for 3 runs with N points:

Average time:

Estimate of time for 2N points:

Give times for 2 runs with 2N points:

Estimate of time for 4N points:

Give times for 2 runs with 4N points:

Do you think the theoretical estimate was fairly accurate or not?

Exercise 6.15. A Mystery Sort

Which algorithm did you choose?

Smallest number of points that requires 3 seconds (N points):

Give times for 3 runs with N points:

Average time:

Estimate of time for 2N points assuming algorithm is $\theta(n^2)$:

Estimate of time for 2N points assuming algorithm is $\theta(n \text{ Lg } n)$:

Give times for 2 runs with 2N points:

What do you believe is the most likely classification for this algorithm?

Exercise 6.16. Timing selection sort

Smallest number of points that requires 3 seconds (N points):

Give times for 3 runs with N points:

Average time:

Estimate of time for 2N points:

Give times for 2 runs with 2N points:

Do you think the theoretical estimate was fairly accurate or not?

Lab Experience 7

Logic Circuits

Objectives

In this lab experience, you will work with a simple logic circuit simulator. The simulator provides capabilities for designing and testing combinational circuits involving AND gates, OR gates, and NOT gates. With the simulator, you will be able to create graphical representations of the gates, place them in desired locations, connect them to form circuits, provide inputs through the use of binary switches, and observe the circuit outputs as the inputs are changed. Once you have become familiar with the behavior of some circuits, you will be asked to modify them and construct truth tables for them.

Background

Figure 7.1 shows the various circuit components you will use in the exercises.

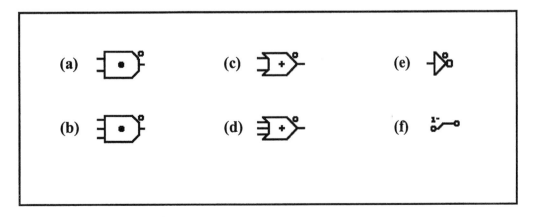

Figure 7.1 Circuit Components.

(a) 2-input AND gate   (c) 2-input OR gate   (e) NOT gate

(b) 3-input AND gate   (d) 3-input OR gate   (f) binary switch

In part (a) of Figure 7.1 is the icon for a 2-input AND gate. The small lines at the left of the icon are the connection points for input lines to the gate. Only one input line can be connected to a given connection point. The line attached to the right of the icon is the connection point for output lines from the gate. You may connect as many output lines to this point as you like. The circle at the upper right of the icon is actually the number zero. This indicates the value of the output of the gate. The value would change to 1 if the two input lines to the gate have values of 1. Part (b) shows a 3-input AND gate. This gate takes three input lines and produces an output of 1 only if all three inputs have values of 1. This gate could be replaced by two 2-input AND gates, but provides for simpler circuit diagrams. Parts (c) and (d) are the corresponding OR gates, and part (e) is the NOT gate with one input and with the opposite value for the output. Part (f) shows a *binary switch* that provides a single output line with the current value of the switch. The value of the switch changes from 0 to 1 or 1 to 0 when we click on the switch.

Components can be connected by clicking on the output connection point of one component and then clicking on an unused input connection point of another component. When you click on the output connection point, you should see the message "Connection to output area" in the status pane at the bottom of the window. This indicates that this connection has been made. The message appears for a few seconds and then goes away. If this message does not appear, try the connection again making sure that you have the cross hairs of the connection tool meeting at the connection point. Similarly, when you click on the input of the target gate, the message "Connection to input area" should temporarily appear at the bottom of the window. Sometimes you can improve the appearance of your circuit by connecting components in stages. Rather than click on the output connection of one gate and then the input connection of another gate and letting the software choose a path for the connecting line, you can first click on the output connection and then click on a succession of intermediate points before clicking on the input connection of the target gate. For example, you might click on the output connection, then click on an intermediate point to the right of the output connection, then on an intermediate point straight above this point and then on the input connection to achieve something like what is shown in Figure 7.2. This method is more useful when the circuits are complicated.

You should now run the lab software package and click the **Logic Circuits** button.

The example circuit

In this exercise, you will work with a circuit that has already been constructed. To get started, select **Open** under the **File** menu and then choose the file **example.cir** (Figures 7.2). You should now see the circuit shown in Figure 7.3. Notice that both switches are originally in the 0 position.

Figure 7.2 Opening a Circuit File.

Figure 7.3 The Example Circuit.

The output value of the upper NOT gate is 1 since its input value from the upper switch is 0. The output value of the lower NOT gate is 1 since its input from the lower switch is 0. The input values to the AND gate are 0 from the upper switch and 1 from the lower NOT gate. Thus, the output value of the AND gate is 0. The inputs to the OR gate are 1 from the upper NOT gate and 0 from the AND gate. The output value of the OR gate is therefore 1. This would be considered the output for the circuit for this setting of the two switches.

To set the values of the switches, select **Set Switch** from the **Changes** menu:

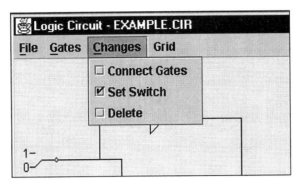

Figure 7.4 Preparing to Set Switches.

Now you can change or toggle the value on any switch by clicking on it.

Exercise 7.1. Truth table for the example circuit

Using A and B to denote the switches, on the Worksheet, fill in the truth table for the circuit by trying each setting of the switches and recording the output value of the circuit.

Exercise 7.2. A slight change in the example circuit

If you inadvertently made any changes to the example circuit, reload Example.cir. Now we will experiment with changing the OR gate to an AND gate. First, it will help to keep track of where the gates are by locating them within a rectangular grid. To display the grid, select **On** from the **Grid** menu. Then choose **Delete** from the **Changes** menu. Now you can delete any gate or switch in your circuit by clicking on it. Click on the OR gate. The gate together with the lines coming into it should disappear. Next, select **And Gate** from the **Gates** menu. Click in the area previously occupied by the OR gate. You should see an AND gate appear in the grid cell where you clicked. Choose **Connect Gates** from the **Changes** menu. Now you can connect any gates and switches in the circuit, as long as connections between them are allowed. Click on the output line of the NOT gate and then the upper input line of the AND gate. Connect the output line of the lower AND gate to the lower input line of the new AND gate. When you are finished editing the circuit, you can hide the grid by choosing **On** from the **Grid** menu. Fill in the truth table for the resulting circuit on the Worksheet by observing the output for each setting of the input switches. In case you might need this circuit later, you can save it, say as Example2.cir, by taking the **Save** option under the **File** menu.

Exercise 7.3. Another change

Now, starting with the circuit which resulted from Exercise 7.2, change the original AND gate to an OR gate, and fill in the truth table for the resulting circuit. You might want to save this circuit as Example3.cir.

Exercise 7.4. A simpler version of the example circuit

There is a simpler circuit that will produce the same outputs as the demo circuit, the original Example.cir. Such a circuit can be made with a single 2-input AND gate and a single NOT gate. Choose

New from the **File** menu and elect to delete the current circuit. The entire circuit should disappear. Display the grid. Choose **Switch** from the **Gates** menu, and place switches in the first and third cells of the leftmost column in the grid. Finally, drop an AND gate and a NOT gate into grid cells somewhere to the right of the switches, and hide the grid. Now experiment with various ways of connecting the components until you find a circuit giving the same truth table as the original example circuit. To try different ways of connecting the gates, you can delete lines and then reconnect the gates and switches. Draw the simpler circuit on the Worksheet.

Exercise 7.5. A one-bit equality circuit

The one-bit equality circuit outputs a 1 just in case both of its inputs are the same and a 0 otherwise. The design of this circuit is discussed in Section 4.4.3 of the text, and the resulting circuit is shown in Figure 4-17 of the text and in Figure 7.5 below. Construct and test such a circuit with the simulator. Give the output values in the truth table on the Worksheet.

Figure 7.5 One-bit equality circuit.

Worksheet
Lab Experience 7
Logic Circuits

Name: _____

Course: _____

Exercise 7.1. Truth table for the example circuit

A	B	Output Value
0	0	
0	1	
1	0	
1	1	

Exercise 7.2. A slight change in the example circuit

A	B	Output Value
0	0	
0	1	
1	0	
1	1	

Exercise 7.3. Another change

A	B	Output Value
0	0	
0	1	
1	0	
1	1	

Exercise 7.4. A simpler version of the example circuit

Diagram of the simpler circuit:

Exercise 7.5. A one-bit equality circuit

A	B	Output Value
0	0	
0	1	
1	0	
1	1	

Lab Experience 8

Logic Circuits

Objectives

In this lab experience, you will continue working with the logic circuit simulator. However, instead of constructing circuits immediately, you will first design blueprints for them. You will begin by constructing the truth table for a circuit. Then you will use the sum-of-products algorithm discussed in Chapter 4 of the text to derive a Boolean expression from the table. Finally, you will use the Boolean expression to construct the corresponding logic circuit with the simulator. In the process, you will see how computer scientists use logic to design hardware.

Exercise 8.1. Sum-of-products for the example circuit

Starting with the truth table of Exercise 7.1 of the lab manual and given below, apply the sum-of-products algorithm to obtain a Boolean expression for another circuit that would provide the same outputs as the example circuit. Then construct the new circuit with the simulator. Note how many more gates would be required for this circuit than appear in the original example circuit. After you have tested the circuit, give the Boolean expression and make a neat drawing of the circuit on the Worksheet.

A	B	Output Value
0	0	1
0	1	1
1	0	1
1	1	0

Exercise 8.2. Two-input parity bit circuit

An *odd parity bit* (see Exercise 16 of Chapter 4 of the text) is an extra bit, attached to the end of a string of bits, which is set to 1 or 0 in such a way that the entire string, including the parity bit, contains an odd number of 1's. For example, if the original string of bits is 01101010, then the parity bit should be a 1, yielding the result 011010101 with an odd number of 1's. If the original string is 100110, the parity bit is 0 since the original string already has an odd number of 1's. In this exercise, design and test a circuit that produces as its output value the correct odd parity bit to accompany two one-bit input values. In other words, the original sting has two bits, one bit for each input value. The final string will have three bits consisting of the two one-bit inputs and the one-bit output from the circuit. Thus the output value should be 1 in the case where both inputs are 0 and in the case where both inputs are 1. Fill in the truth table on the Worksheet, apply the Sum of Products algorithm to derive the Boolean expression, construct the circuit, and finally test it. Give the Boolean expression and a neat drawing of the circuit on the Worksheet.

Exercise 8.3. Three-input parity bit circuit

Following the design technique of the first two exercises, construct and test a three-bit parity circuit.

Exercise 8.4. Bits as operation codes

Later in the course, you will study in some depth how certain bits in computer instructions are used as codes to let the computer know which operation to perform. For example, one code might indicate that an addition should be performed, while another code might indicate that a compare for equality should be performed. In this exercise, you will design, construct and test a circuit that performs this kind of function. Your circuit will have three inputs and a single output. The first two inputs are used as codes to indicate what should be done to the third input to produce the output. There are four possibilities for the two-bit codes, 00, 01,10, and 11. We'll use the codes as follows:

(1)   If the first two input values are 0 (code 00), the output should be 0, no matter what the third input is. Here the function of the circuit becomes a set-to-zero function on the third input.

(2)   If the first input is 0 and the second is 1 (code 01), the output should be the same as the third input. The function of the circuit is the identity function on the third input.

(3)   If the first input is 1 and the second is 0 (code 10), the output should be the negation of the third input.

(4)   If the first two inputs are 1 (code 11), the output should be 1 no matter what the third input is. The function is a set-to-one operation.

Make a truth table that gives the appropriate output values according to this discussion, write the corresponding Boolean expression, construct the circuit with the simulator, and test the circuit by checking the output values for each setting of the switches.

Worksheet
Lab Experience 8
Logic Circuits

Name: _____

Course: _____

Exercise 8.1. Sum-of-products for the example circuit

Boolean expression for new version of the example circuit:

Circuit diagram for the new version of the example circuit:

Exercise 8.2. Two-input parity bit circuit

A	B	Odd Parity Bit
0	0	
0	1	
1	0	
1	1	

Boolean expression of two-input parity circuit:

Circuit diagram for two-input parity circuit:

Exercise 8.3. Three-input parity bit circuit

A	B	C	Odd Parity Bit
0	0	0	
0	0	1	
0	1	0	
0	1	1	
1	0	0	
1	0	1	
1	1	0	
1	1	1	

Boolean expression of three-input parity circuit:

Circuit diagram for three-input parity circuit:

Exercise 8.4. Bits as operation codes

A (code bit 1)	B (code bit 2)	C	Result
0	0	0	
0	0	1	
0	1	0	
0	1	1	
1	0	0	
1	0	1	
1	1	0	
1	1	1	

Boolean expression:

Circuit diagram:

Lab Experience 9

von Neumann Machines

Objectives

This laboratory experience will introduce you to the operation of a simple von Neumann machine. You will load some prewritten machine language programs into a simulator and observe the behavior of the machine as you step through each instruction in a program. After you have become familiar with the structure and behavior of the machine, you will be asked to make some minor changes to the sample programs, run them again, and make comments on their effects. In the process, you will be placed in much the same position as that of the first computer programmers, who had to enter each machine language instruction by hand. By giving you exposure to a 'bare machine,' we hope that you will appreciate the extent to which the programming process becomes automated in later lab sections.

Background

As you learned in Chapter 5 of the text, von Neumann machines have a finite amount of memory for storing program instructions and data. They also have a collection of registers for quickly locating important data, such as the address of the next instruction in memory or the contents of the instruction about to be executed. The instructions and data in a von Neumann machine are represented as strings of binary digits-- machine code in the conventional sense. Finally, each instruction is executed in the order in which it is found in memory, unless a jump instruction causes control to branch around a series of instructions to some other location in memory.

The architecture and instruction set of our machine closely resemble those described in Chapter 5 of the text. Each instruction consists of two parts: a four-bit opcode that represents the operation to be performed, and a twelve-bit address field that represents the address of the operand. The sixteen binary opcodes and their meanings are shown in table 9.1.

Numeric code	Meaning	
0000	load x	x → R
0001	store x	R → x
0010	clear x	0 → x
0011	add x	R+x → R
0100	increment x	x+1 → x
0101	subtract x	R-x → R
0110	decrement x	x-1 → x

0111	compare x	if x>R then
		    100 → CCR
		elseif x<R then
		    001 → CCR
		elseif x=R then
		    010 → CCR

1000	jump x	goto x
1001	jumpgt x	goto x if CCR=100
1010	jumpeq x	goto x if CCR=010
1011	jumplt x	goto x if CCR=001
1100	jumpneq x	goto x if CCR<>010
1101	in x	store input in x
1110	out x	output x
1111	halt	

Table 9.1 Binary opcodes and their meanings

The machine consists of 4096 (exactly 4K) cells of memory. Each cell contains sixteen bits. If a cell contains a machine language instruction, then the leftmost four bits represent the opcode, and the remaining twelve bits represent the address of the operand. If a cell contains a machine language datum, then the leftmost bit represents the sign bit of a fifteen-bit integer (0 = '+', 1 = '-'), and the remaining fifteen bits represent the integer's absolute value.

At the level of machine code, data and instructions all look the same. For example, suppose that the contents of the tenth cell in memory is the binary string '1000000000000111.' If we view this string as an instruction, the leftmost four bits ('1000') represent the opcode for **jump**, while the remaining twelve bits represent the address of the operand (the destination of the jump).   Put simply, the instruction says 'jump to location number 7' (actually, to the eighth cell in memory, because we start at location zero). If we view this string as data, however, we have a sixteen-bit signed integer value, namely, -7 (the leftmost bit denotes '-', while the remaining fifteen bits represent 7).

To run the von Neumann machine simulator, select **von Neumann Machine** from the lab software menu. The von Neumann machine is displayed as a group of several panes on the screen (Figure 9.1):

Figure 9.1 von Neumann machine simulator.

In the exercises that follow, you will not be asked to enter an entire machine language program by hand. Instead, you will load some sample programs provided with the lab software, and run them to observe their behavior.

Exercise 9.1 Adding two numbers and displaying the result

Begin by selecting **Open** from the **File** menu. You should search for the file **Example1.mac** in the **Examples** folder, and then load it by clicking **OK**. If all goes well, you should see the first machine language program in memory:

Figure 9.2 Example1.mac loaded into memory.

Click the **Reset** button, and notice that a bar appears over the first machine language instruction in memory. Let's interpret this instruction. The opcode is 0000 which indicates a load instruction. The address is 000000000101 which is binary for decimal 5. Thus the instruction should load the value stored at address 5 into the register R. Memory location 5 contains a binary two. So an appropriate interpretation for this instruction would be "The value 2 stored in location 5 is to be loaded into R." Now on the Worksheet copy down the binary form of this instruction and the interpretation of what the instruction should do when executed. Next, click the step button. This will execute the first instruction. Note what happens to the contents of the registers, and the movement of the black bar to the next instruction. Now repeat the process of writing down the instruction and your interpretation of it, and stepping through it, until a message box appears that signals the halting of the program. If you need help, look in Table 9.1, or click on the **Opcodes** button. On the Worksheet, give the main function of the program. Tell whether or not there is any output in the output window.

Exercise 9.2 Editing memory to use different data

Based on what you saw in the first exercise, where are the data for the program located? On the Worksheet, give the memory addresses where the data (as opposed to the instructions) are located. You will now run the program again with different data. To place a new datum in a memory cell, select the desired cell and click the **Edit** button. Do that now for the first **data** cell of the program. You should see cell editor box that displays the current contents of the cell (Figure 9.4):

Figure 9.4 Entering new data into memory cell.

Enter the number 7 in binary form. Then move to the next data cell and enter the number 8 in binary form. Finally, reset the machine and run the program by clicking **Run** this time. Did you receive the expected output? Indicate the output on the Worksheet.

Exercise 9.3. Getting data from the user

A better way to test programs with different data is to allow the user to enter the data during program execution. Moreover, it would be nice if the user could enter data in user-friendly form, such as decimal notation for integer values. Load the file **Example2.mac** from the **Examples** folder and reset the machine. Write down your interpretations of the first three instructions (Worksheet). Now step through the program. When you are prompted for input data, enter some two-digit decimal numbers, like 34 and 76.

Exercise 9.4. Making choices by comparison and jump

You will recall from the discussion of algorithms in the first three chapters of the text that we can test data for certain properties and make a decision about which statements to execute as a result of what we find. Suppose we want to display the smaller of two input values. The algorithm might compare the two numbers and, if the first is smaller than the second, then display the first; otherwise, the algorithm will display the second. To observe this algorithm as a machine language program, load the file **Example3.mac** from the **Examples** folder. Reset the machine and run the program a couple of times with different input values to get a sense that it does what it is supposed to do. For each of the instructions up to the halt instruction, write down the instruction and your interpretation of the instruction. Then reset and step through the execution of the program using 5 for the first input value and 7 for the second input value. Record on the Worksheet the address of the instruction being executed and the values stored in the top four registers (pc, ir, r and ccr) immediately after executing the instruction. What happened to the **ccr** register after the comparison took place (Worksheet)? Did the machine execute one **jump** instruction, or two (Worksheet)? Now reset and repeat the procedure using 7 for the first input value and 5 for the second input value.

Exercise 9.5. Looping by comparison and jump

Recall from the text that many algorithms require that a block of instructions be run repeatedly, until a condition becomes true (you have been doing this yourself in the previous exercises--interpreting and stepping through an instruction, until the program halts). For example, we might want to input an arbitrary number of numbers and compute and display their average. We would first input the number of numbers expected, save this value in an extra memory location for a counter, and set a running total to zero. Then, we would input a number, add it to the running total, and subtract one from the counter, until the counter became zero. After the loop was finished, we would divide the total by the number of numbers expected and display the result.

A simpler algorithm that illustrates looping in machine language is in the file **Example4.mac**. Load that program now. The algorithm displays all of the integer values between an input value and 1 inclusive, assuming that the input value is greater than 0. Run the program once to verify that this is the case. Then step through it to observe the behavior of the loop more closely. Write down your interpretation of each instruction as you make the first pass through the loop (Worksheet). What would happen if the input value were zero? What would happen if the input value were a negative number? (*Caution*: if you find that you cannot stop the run of a program by selecting the **Stop** button, try the **Ctrl-Break** command on your keyboard, and then **Stop**).

Exercise 9.6. An error: integer overflow

We will take your data from Exercise 1 and put an error into it to illustrate an important point about von Neumann machines. Load the file Example1.mac. Edit either of the data cells in the program, so that the value in one of them is '0111111111111111.' This is the largest positive integer that can be represented by sixteen-bit signed magnitude notation. What do you suppose should happen when the machine tries to add a positive number to this value? The best way to see is to run the program. Be sure that the other number is greater than zero (1 will do just fine). The program should halt at the addition instruction with an error message. This is an example of an error for integer overflow. The nice thing about this error is that the machine finds it for you and tells you exactly what it is and where it occurs. Integer overflow occurs when the machine cannot represent the result of an arithmetic calculation in the given amount of memory. In the case of our machine, the magnitude or absolute value of the number must not exceed 32767.

Exercise 9.7. Observing fetch, decode, and execute

Recall from Chapter 5 that stepping through each machine language instruction involves three phases: fetch, decode, and execute. The first two phases, fetch and decode, are the same for every instruction. Briefly, fetch copies the address from program counter (PC) to the memory address register (MAR). This address is then used to fetch the contents of the instruction, which is placed in the memory data register (MDR). The instruction is copied from the MDR to the instruction register (IR). Finally, the address in the PC is incremented by 1. The decode phase extracts the four-bit opcode from the instruction in the IR, and sends it to the instruction decoder. The third phase, execute, is different for each instruction. For example, executing the instruction load x consists of three steps: (1) extract the address of x from the IR and copy it to the MAR; (2) fetch the contents at this address and copy it into the MDR; and (3) copy the contents of the MDR into the data register (R). To observe the fetch/decode/execute cycle, load the file **Example1.mac** into memory and select **On** from the **Step Into** menu:

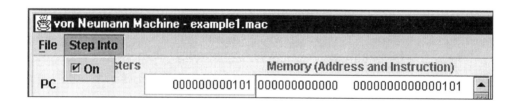

Figure 9.5 Turning on Step Into.

As long as this item is checked, you will be able to step through a program but not run it. As you step into each instruction in memory, a description of the fetch cycle pops up in the pane at the lower right of the window. Each click of the step button now moves the black bar down through the instructions in the fetch cycle. Note the changes in the MAR and MDR as you go. When you get to the execute phase, you may see changes to the ALU registers as well. If you wish to turn off this feature so that you can step through a program more quickly or run it, just select **On** from **Step Into** again.

Worksheet
Lab Experience 9
von Neumann Machines

Name: _____

Course: _____

Exercise 9.1 Adding two numbers and displaying the result

Instruction	Interpretation

Main function of the program:

Any output in output window:

Exercise 9.2 Editing memory to use different data

Output of run with new data:

Exercise 9.3. Getting data from the user

Instruction	Interpretation

Exercise 9.4. Making choices by comparison and jump

Address	Instruction	Interpretation
0		
1		
2		
3		
4		
5		
6		
7		
8		

Stepping with first input value 5 and second input value 7:

Address	pc	ir	r	ccr

What happened to value in ccr?

How many jumps were executed?

Stepping with first input value 7and second input value 5:

Address	pc	ir	r	ccr

What happened to value in ccr?

How many jumps were executed?

Exercise 9.5. Looping by comparison and jump

Address	Instruction	Interpretation
0		
1		
2		
3		
4		
5		
6		
7		
8		

Lab Experience 10

Assembly Language Programming

Objectives

This lab experience will introduce you to programming in assembly language. You will load some sample programs provided with the lab software, assemble and run them, and make some simple changes to them to become familiar with the language. Then you will solve some problems by writing some assembly language programs from scratch.

Background

In the previous lab experience, you became acquainted with the structure and function of a simple von Neumann machine. You also experienced some of the same difficulties that the first programmers had in programming in machine language. You would probably agree that the solution of even a simple problem such as adding two numbers together and displaying the result required a great deal of thinking and planning. The problem is not in knowing what has to be done, but in translating your strategy into the unfamiliar notation of the binary machine code. When it comes to solving slightly more complex problems, like using addition to multiply two numbers, it helped the first programmers to write out the solution in a low-level pseudo code, and then translate this to the machine code. This technique simplified the programming process, but they still had to do the translation by hand. Even though the translation from the lower-level pseudo code to the machine code was fairly simple and straightforward, it was still prone to human error (typing in the wrong machine address for an instruction or data label, or typing in the wrong numeric opcode for the name of an operation).

It turns out that the process of translating from a low-level pseudo code to machine code is so simple and mechanical that a computer professional can write a program to do that for us. Then we just enter our program in the low-level pseudo code and the translator converts it to an equivalent machine language program. The low-level pseudo code is called assembly language, and the translator is called an *assembler*.

As you will recall from Chapter 6 of the text, the advantages of programming in assembly language instead of machine code are obvious:

83

1. You can work with mnemonic names for operations, data, and the locations of instructions, such as **add, result**, and **endwhile**.   You no longer have to worry about figuring out or remembering the binary representations of addresses or opcodes.

2. The assembler can guarantee that data is kept separate from instructions in the machine code. You just enter the instructions in the assembly language program first, and then the data.

3. The assembler can catch many errors that would otherwise have been detected only at run-time. For example, it is possible to write a machine language instruction that jumps to a data location in memory. The assembler can stop the translation of your program and force you to fix this bug before the program ever runs. A list of these errors can be found at the end of this lab.

By automating the program translation process, an assembler provides a layer of virtual machine between you and the computer, thus making problem solving less tedious and more powerful.

To run the assembler, click **Assembler** on the main software menu. You will be presented with two panes (Figure 10.1).

Figure 10.1   The assembler panes.

The left pane is intended for the entry of assembly language source programs. The right pane is a utility window for displaying program listings during compilation, symbol tables, and object code. You also have the following menus:

1. **File.** From this menu, you can **Save** and **Open** assembly language source programs or obtain a **New** entry pane. You can also print a listing of the program after it assembles.

2. **Edit.** The standard Windows editing operations for a text pane.

3. **Assembler.** From this menu, the user can **Assemble** the source program, **View the symbol table** that is generated during translation (you will do this in Lab Experience 15), and **View the object code.** The user can also **Execute** the object code, which actually loads the object code into a von Neumann machine simulator.

Exercise 10.1. Adding two numbers and displaying the result

Select **Open** from the **File** menu and select the file **Example1.asm** in the **Examples** folder. Now click the **OK** button. The text of an assembly language source program should appear in the source program pane. You will recall that you loaded an equivalent machine language program in the Lab Experience 9. Study the code to verify that the program will do what your machine language program did (if it ran correctly!). Then choose **Assemble** from the **Assembler** menu. You will see a program listing appear in the utility pane. The listing is just a copy of the source program, with each line numbered for your reference. At the end of the listing, there should be a message that assembly has been completed without syntax errors. The assembler panes should look like those in Figure 10.2.

Figure 10.2   A sample assembly language program and its listing.

The assembler has instantly done what you so painstakingly had to figure out yourself in the last lab section: translate some thoughts expressed in English-like code to the same thoughts expressed in machine code. To see that this is the case, select **View Object Code** from the **Assembler** menu. The machine language instructions corresponding to the source code will be displayed in the utility pane, as in Figure 10.3.

Figure 10.3   Machine code for an assembly language program.

Finally, run the program by selecting **Execute** from the **Assembler** menu. A von Neumann machine simulator pops up, with the machine code of our program loaded into memory and the source code displayed in the source pane. When you run the program in the simulator (by selecting either **Run** or **Step**), the current instruction is selected in both forms of the program. Run the program and indicate the output on the Worksheet.

Exercise 10.2. Some syntax errors

You will typically begin by entering a source program by hand or opening it from a file. **Assemble** is the only option available from the **Assembler** menu at this point. During assembly, the system displays a program listing and any syntax error messages in the utility pane. Each line of source text is numbered in the listing for easy reference, and an error message appears more or less on the line following the line of code in which the error occurs. Assembly halts at the first error. Error detection is pretty thorough: errors are caught even at the lexical level, such as illegal labels and integer literals that are too large for sixteen-bit sign magnitude representation.

The assembler generates the following syntax error messages:

```
.begin expected.
.end expected.
Illegal opcode: <symbol>
Halt does not take operand.
Wrong number of fields in instruction.
Label must end with :
Label already used: <symbol>
Undeclared data label: <symbol>
Undeclared instruction label: <symbol>
Data label already used as instruction label: <symbol>
Data directive already exists for label: <symbol>
Value must be an integer.
Number is too large.
Not enough memory for instructions.
Not enough memory for data.
```

The program that we just loaded from a file had no syntax errors. Let's put some syntax errors into it so that we can see how the assembler detects them.

a. Replace the operand **x** in the first instruction, **load x**, with the operand **a**, and reassemble the program. The assembler should discover that you forgot to provide a data declaration for **a**. The assembler forces you to keep track of all of your data and their initial values by declaring them at the bottom of the program. Correct this error before going on.

b. Replace the operator **add** with the operator **multiply** in the second instruction. The assembler should discover an unrecognized opcode. Correct this error before going on.

c. Replace the number 2 with the number 40000 in the first data declaration. Note the error detected by the assembler. Correct this error before going on.

d. Delete the space between **add** and **y** in the second instruction. Note the error detected. There must be at least one blank space or tab between an operator and its operand. Correct this error before going on.

e. Insert a carriage return after the second instruction. Note the error detected. Assembly language typically has a *fixed format*, which requires an instruction to appear on each line of a program. Correct this error before going on.

f. Insert a blank space, followed by **subtract**, at the end of the second line. Note the error detected. Since the instruction has three lexical items, the assembler expects the first one to be a label ending with a colon (:). Don't correct this error yet.

g. Oblige the assembler by inserting a colon (:) after **add** (be sure that there are no blank spaces between the colon and the **d**). Note the error detected. Now change **y** to **add**. The assembler treats **subtract** as an undeclared data label, which you could remedy by declaring it at the bottom of the program.

Exercise 10.3. Making decisions in assembly language

Open the file **Example2.asm** and study the program. What does it do? Assemble and execute the program. Does it behave as expected? Modify the program so that it displays the larger of the two numbers, and test it until it behaves correctly.

Exercise 10.4. Loops in assembly language

Open the file **Example3.asm** and study the program. What does it do? Assemble and execute the program. Does it behave as expected? Modify the program so that it checks to see that the input data is greater than zero before it starts the loop. If that's not the case, the program should halt with no output.

Exercise 10.5. Larger/Smaller

Write pseudocode for a program which allows the user to input two numbers (X and Y) and a code C. If the code has value 1, the program should output the larger of X and Y and otherwise output the smaller.

Now convert your pseudocode to an assembly language program. Enter the program into the lab software assembler. Assemble the program and execute it with different input data.

Exercise 10.6. Even/odd

Write pseudocode for a program which allows the user to input a positive number N. The program should output 1 if the number is odd and output 0 if the number is even. (*Hint*: keep subtracting 2 from N until .....)

Exercise 10.7. Multiplication

Our assembly language has no operator for multiplication. But multiplication can be performed by repeatedly adding one number to a running total, and reducing the other number by one, until the second number becomes zero. Write and test an assembly language program that displays the product of two input numbers.

Worksheet
Lab Experience 10
Assembly Language Programming

Name: _____

Course: _____

Exercise 10.1. Adding two numbers and displaying the result

Output from running the program:

Exercise 10.2. Some syntax errors

    a. Error message:

    b. Error message:

    c. Error message:

    d. Error message:

    e. Error message:

    f. Error message:

    g. First error message:

        Second error message:

Exercise 10.3. Making decisions in assembly language

What is the main function of Example2?

Write your program to give the larger of two numbers:

Exercise 10.4. Loops in assembly language

What is the main function of Example2?

Program:

Exercise 10.5. Larger/Smaller

Program for larger/smaller:

Exercise 10.6. Even/odd

Program for even/odd:

Exercise 10.7. Multiplication

Program for multiplication:

Lab Experience 11

Java Programming – Input, Output, and Control Structures

Objectives

In Chapter 5 of the text, you learned that the first programmers wrote programs directly (and, perhaps, painfully!) in machine language. In Chapter 6, you learned that a programming language translator, called an assembler, can ease the burden of writing programs. Assembly language resembles a low-level pseudo code, in which we can express algorithms in terms that are more intelligible to a human being. However, as problems get more complex, the assembly language programs that might solve them become difficult to understand as well. Even a fairly simple problem, such as writing a loop to multiply two numbers, requires us to design a solution in high-level pseudo code before translating by hand to a form resembling an assembly language program. Even if we think that our high-level design is correct, we face the additional problem of manual translation from high-level pseudo code to assembly language.

This lab section will introduce you to a tool that allows you to write a program directly in a language that resembles a high-level pseudo code. The tool, called a compiler, translates programs written in a language called Java to a form that can be executed on a machine. Actually, the compiler does not support the translation of all of the features you will find in Java; but a large subset of them is covered. The compiler supports the "procedural" subset of Java discussed in Chapter 7 of the text. The syntax rules for our Java appear at the end of this lab. You will see that you can solve fairly complex problems easily and quickly in Java. In the process, you should appreciate the extent to which several layers of virtual machine free you from low-level concerns and permit you to think like a human being once again.

Background

In this lab, we examine Java programs that are similar to those discussed early in Chapter 7 of the text. Each program in this lab has the following structure:

```
public class <class name> {

    public static void main(String[] args){
        data declarations
        statements
    }
}
```

The expression `<class name>` should be the name of the Java source program file to the left of the dot. Thus, if the Java source file is named **Example1.java**, the class name should be **Example1**. Note that Java is case sensitive, so the name **Example1** is different from the name **example1** (both as a file name and as a Java class name).

In contrast to assembly language programs, Java programs typically declare data before stating the instructions. Moreover, there are several kinds of data declarations and statements in Java. To help you keep this straight, the compiler is pretty fussy about the syntax or form of each kind of declaration and statement. You will learn the different kinds of data declarations and statements in Java by running some example programs provided with the software. Remember to keep the syntax rules and notes on our subset of Java (at the end of this lab) handy.

Your school might already have one of the many excellent commercially available environments, such as Borland JBuilder, Symantec Visual Café, or Metrowerks CodeWarrior. These can be used to edit, compile, and run Java programs. If you do not have access to one of these environments, we recommend the following tools and use them in our discussion below:

- The language translation lab software can be used just to edit and transfer Java source files to and from disk.
- The JDK from Sun can be used to compile and run Java programs (see installation instructions in the Preface to this manual).

Regardless of the tools you use to work with Java, you should put the files **Console.class** and **LabFrame.class** in the folder where your Java programs are. They already are in the **Examples** folder.

Exercise 11.1. Adding two integers and displaying the result

Click the button **Language Translation** on the main menu and then select **Java** from the **Language** menu. Open the file **Example1.java** from the **File** menu. Your window should now look like the one depicted in Figure 11.1.

```
// Example1.java

public class Example1{

   public static void main(String[] args){
      final int first = 4;
      final int second = 5;
      int sum;
      sum = first + second;
      System.out.println(sum);
   }

}
```

Figure 11.1 Viewing the first Java source program.

This program does exactly what the first example assembly language program did in Lab Experience 10. It defines two integer data values, adds them together, and displays their sum. Note that the data are defined as constants in Java. Note also that the sum is defined as a variable.

To compile this program, open a terminal window and move to the **Examples** directory. Then type the command **javac Example1.java** at the prompt and press Enter. The program should compile without errors (see Figure 11.2).

```
MS-DOS

C:\>cd invitation\examples

C:\Invitation\EXAMPLES>javac Example1.java

C:\Invitation\EXAMPLES>
```

Figure 11.2 Compiling a Java program.

Now run the program by typing **java Example1** and pressing Enter at the prompt. The program should run and display the output in the terminal window (Figure 11.3).

Figure 11.3 Running a Java program.

Note that the command **javac** expects the full file name (with the **.java** extension) whereas the command **java** expects the file name without the **.java** extension.

Exercise 11.2 Dealing with syntax errors

The syntax of Java is more complex than the syntax of assembly language. For this reason, beginning programmers frequently make syntax errors until they become acquainted with the language. When a syntax error occurs, the compiler displays an informative error message. In fact, several error messages may appear. You should focus on the first few and try to understand those. In **Example1.java**, suppose we misspell the variable sum as su in the statement sum = first + second;. We then save and compile the program. Figure 11.4 shows the syntax error messages and the lines of code in which they occur.

Figure 11.4 Java syntax error messages.

Edit the output statement in your program, save the program to the file, and compile it so that this syntax error occurs. Then fix the error, save the file, and recompile. Now force another syntax error by changing the + sign to the $ symbol and recompile. Write a short paragraph that explains the error messages in the Worksheet.

Exercise 11.3 Labeling output

Edit the output statement so that the output will be labeled. For example, you might say

```
System.out.println("The sum is " + sum);
```

Recompile and execute the program, until you are satisfied with the output. Enter your changes on the Worksheet.

Exercise 11.4. Displaying the sum of two input integers

Open the file **Example2.java** from the **File** menu. This program is like **Example1.java**, but allows the user to enter the data as inputs from the keyboard. Note that the data are defined as variables rather than constants. Note also that the user is prompted for input before each input statement. Compile and execute the program.

Exercise 11.5. Computing the area of a triangle

Open the file **Example3.java** from the **File** menu. This program computes and displays the area of a triangle, after the user has entered the height and base. Note that the height, base, and area are declared as doubles (real numbers) rather than integers. Compile and execute the program. Run it with two sets of test data.

Exercise 11.6. Converting degrees Fahrenheit to degrees centigrade

Design, code, and test a Java program that takes degrees Fahrenheit from the user and displays the same temperature in degrees centigrade. Be sure to label the output descriptively. The formula for the conversion is

```
centigrade = (fahrenheit - 32) * 5 / 9
```

Enter your program on the Worksheet.

Exercise 11.7. The **if** statement

Open the file **Example4.java** from the **File** menu. You should see a program that displays the absolute value of an input number. To solve this problem, we prompt the user for a value. If the value is less than 0, then we negate it and store it back in the variable. Finally, we output the value. Note that the negation only occurs if the condition in the **if** statement is true.   If the condition is false, we go on to output the value right away. This is an example of a one-way choice. Compile the program, execute it, and run it with positive and negative inputs.

Exercise 11.8. The **if...else** statement

For this exercise, you will take the preceding program and modify it so that it outputs a message that the value is positive if that is true, or negative otherwise. First, delete the output statement. Then, replace

the line where the number is negated with an output statement for the message that the number is negative. Compile and run the program with positive and negative inputs. What happens? Do we get the expected output in both cases? Now return to the compiler and convert the **if** statement to a two-way decision. Insert the word **else** on the line after the **if** statement. Then, on the next line, indent one tab stop and insert an output statement for the message that the number is positive. Compile and test the program with positive and negative numbers.

Exercise 11.9. A three-way decision

It turns out that the program from the previous exercise still is not quite right. It tells us we entered a positive number when we enter a zero. Therefore, we need three possible messages, including one for the case of zero. To handle this option, we can nest the existing **if** statement in the **else** part of a higher-level **if** statement. This three-way decision should have the following form:

```
if (expression) then
     statement
else if (expression) then
     statement
else
     statement
```

To fix your program from the previous exercise, insert the word **else** in front of the word **if**. Then open up two lines above the first **else**, and insert an **if** statement that will handle the case where the input value is exactly zero. Compile and run the program with all three possible cases of input.

Exercise 11.10. The while statement

Open the file **Example5.java** from the **File** menu. This program illustrates the use of the *while statement* in Java. The program does the same thing as an assembly language program in Lab Experience 10: take an input integer from the user, and display all of the values from that integer down to one. This version of the while statement is known as a *count-controlled loop*. Compile the program and run it with some test values. Now suppose we wanted to display the values in ascending order. Modify the current program so that this is the result.

Exercise 11.11. Accumulating a sum

Modify the program from the previous exercise, so that it displays just the sum of all of the numbers from one to the input number. Be sure to test your program with several inputs.

Exercise 11.12. Accumulating a sum of a series of input values

Modify the program from the previous exercise, so that it displays the sum of a series of input numbers. You should prompt the user for the number of input numbers to be entered, and use this number as your loop counter.

Exercise 11.13. Accumulating a sum of absolute values

Modify the program from the previous exercise, so that it displays the sum of absolute values of a series of input numbers. That is, it should display the same result whether the input values are negative or positive.

Syntax Rules of Java as Covered in Labs 11-13

For the full definition of the Java language, see the documentation on Sun's Web site. We use an extended Backus-Naur grammar to pick out the subset of Java used in labs 11-13. This grammar has three kinds of symbols:

1. **Terminal symbols**. These symbols are enclosed in double quotes. Examples are "+" and "main". These symbols are reserved words and operator symbols, and make up the vocabulary of the language.
2. **Non-terminal** symbols. These symbols designate phrases in the language that must be defined further. Examples are methodCall and constantDeclaration.
3. **Metasymbols**. The grammar uses these symbols to form rules. The metasymbols appear in the following table:

Metasymbol	Use in a rule
=	Means is defined as.
|	Separates alternative choices.
{ }	Enclose items that can appear zero or more times.
[ ]	Enclose an optional item.
( )	Enclose items that should be grouped as a unit.

The rules are formed by placing the defined symbol to the left and its definition to the right of the = symbol. For example, the rule

```
expression = simpleExpression [ relationalOperator simpleExpression ]
```

is read as "An expression is defined as a simple expression, which may or may not be followed by a relational operator and a simple expression." An example of an expression in a Java program is **x >= y**.

The rule

```
simpleExpression = term { addingOperator term }
```

is read as "A simple expression is defined as a term, followed by zero or more adding operators and terms." An example of a simple expression in a Java program is **x + y - z**.

As in English and other natural languages, every phrase in a Java program must follow a syntax rule. If you have trouble understanding the compiler's syntax error messages, check the grammar and the list of error messages that follow.

```
program = { functionDeclaration } mainFunction

mainMethod = "public" "static" "void" "main" "("String[] args")" block

block = "{" { constantDeclaration } { variableDeclaration }
```

```
       { statement } "}"

constantDeclaration = "final" ( "int" | "double" ) identifier "="
                      ( integer | double ) ";"

variableDeclaration = ( "int" | "double" | "char" ) identifierList ";"

identifierList = identifier [ "[" integerConstant "]" ]
               { "," identifier [ "[" integerConstant "]" ] }

integerConstant = integer | identifier

methodDeclaration = methodHeading block

methodHeading = "static" returnType identifier
              "(" [ formalParameters ] ")"

returnType = "void" | "int" | "double" | "char"

formalParameters = parameterDeclaration { "," parameterDeclaration }

parameterDeclaration = ( "int" | "double" | "char" )
                       identifier [ "[" "]" ]

statement = ifStatement | whileStatement | returnStatement
          | outputStatement | compoundStatement
          | assignmentStatement | methodCallStatement

ifStatement = "if" "(" expression ")" statement [ "else" statement ]

whileStatement = "while" "(" expression ")" statement

returnStatement = "return" expression ";"

outputStatement = "System.out.println" "(" expression ")" ";"

compoundStatement = "{" { statement } "}"

assignmentStatement = name "=" expression ";"

methodCallStatement = methodCall ";"

methodCall = identifier "(" [ actualParameters ] ")"

actualParameters = expression { "," expression }

expression = simpleExpression [ relationalOperator simpleExpression ]

simpleExpression = term { addingOperator term }

term = factor { multiplyingOperator factor }
```

```
factor = [ "-" | "!" ] primary

primary = integer | double | character | string
          | name | functionCall | "(" expression ")"

name = identifier [ "[" expression "]" ]

relationalOperator = "==" | "!=" | ">" | "<" | ">=" | "<="

addingOperator = "+" | "-"

multiplyingOperator = "*" | "/" | "%"

integer = digit { digit }

double = integer "." integer

identifier = [ "_" ] letter { "_" | letter | digit }

string = """ { any printable character } """

character = "'" any printable character "'"
```

Additional Notes

1. Java is case sensitive. Thus, **main** is a reserved word, but **Main** is an identifier.
2. The primitive data types are **int**, **double**, and **char**.
3. The structured data type is array. The base type of an array can be **int**, **double**, or **char**.
4. Variable declarations must appear within a block.
5. Binary operations (**+**, **-**, etc.) on an **int** and a **double** produce a **double** as a result.
6. An **int** value may be assigned to a **double** variable, input into a **double** variable, or passed as an actual parameter in the place of a **double** formal parameter. In these cases, the **int** value is promoted to a **double** value.
7. When a **char** value is assigned or passed as a parameter to an **int** variable, the character's ASCII value is used.
8. The methods **Console.readInt**, **Console.readDouble**, **Console.readChar**, and **Console.readString** are used to input data of type **int**, **double**, **char**, and **String**, respectively. Each method expects a string as a parameter. This string is displayed as a prompt to the user for input. Each method returns the input datum or throws an exception if the datum is not well-formed (for example, if a number contains letters). There is also a version of **Console.readInt** that does not expect a parameter and can be used in Lab 15.

Worksheet
Lab Experience 11
Java Programming – Input, Output, and Control Structures

Name: _____

Course: _____

Exercise 11.2 Dealing with syntax errors

Exercise 11.3 Labeling output

Exercise 11.6. Converting degrees Fahrenheit to degrees centigrade

Exercise 11.8. The `if...else` statement

Exercise 11.9. A three-way decision

Exercise 11.10. The while statement

Exercise 11.11. Accumulating a sum

Exercise 11.12. Accumulating a sum of a series of input values

Exercise 11.13. Accumulating a sum of absolute values

Lab Experience 12

Java Programming – Methods and Arrays

Objectives

In Lab Experience 11, you used the major control structures of Java: sequencing, selection, and looping. In the current lab experience, you will learn how to design and use Java *methods*. A method is an important *abstraction* mechanism; that is, it captures a frequently used pattern of instructions in a single named entity. You will also learn to define and use *parameters* with methods. Parameters allow a programmer to pass data to a method. Parameters allow a method to describe a general task that can be performed on a set of different instances of a problem.

Finally, you will be introduced to a data structure that appeared in the discussion of the searching, data cleanup, and sorting algorithms of Chapters 2 and 3: the *array*. Arrays are a useful abstraction mechanism for representing lists of data. These features of Java should persuade you that problem solving in a high-level language can be easy and fun.

Exercise 12.1. Methods as abstraction mechanisms

Suppose you want to skip two lines between some outputs. You could accomplish that in a Java program by means of two successive output statements. If you wanted to skip five lines, you could type in five successive output statements. Suppose that you wanted to skip the same number of lines at several places in your program. If it were just two lines at a time, you probably would not object to typing the two output statements on several occasions. However, it would definitely be irritating if you had to type five of them each time. It turns out that there is a way of removing this irritation in a Java program. The language provides a way of packaging a frequently used sequence of statements as a single, abstract unit and giving it a name, say, **skipFiveLines**. Then, wherever you want to skip five lines in this program, you just use this new name, **skipFiveLines**, as easily as you use a single output statement. This abstraction is called a *method*.

To see how a method is defined and used, open the file **Example6.java** from the **File** menu. There you will see a method definition and a use of the method in the program. Compile and run the program to observe the result. Then modify the method so that it skips seven lines rather than five. Test it again.

Exercise 12.2. Generalizing methods with parameters

In general, one might skip any number of lines in an output sequence by typing just that number of output statements in a program. This can be expressed as a *general* problem: perform n output statements, where $n > 0$. We would like a general solution to this problem. However, every time we want our method from the previous exercise to solve this problem for a new case of n, we must rewrite the method itself.

Again, there is a way of providing one method in Java to solve a problem of this kind. We can add a *parameter* to the definition of the method. The parameter, call it **n**, is a number that will specify how many output statements to execute. We can then write the method as a loop from **n** down to one, and we will have a general solution to the problem of skipping *n* lines!

To see how a parameter is defined and used, open the file **Example7.java** from the **File** menu. You will see a method called **skipLines**, with a single *formal parameter*, **n**. When the method is called in a given spot in the program, the programmer can specify how many lines to skip by passing an *actual parameter*, an integer value, to the method. Compile and run the program to verify that it behaves as expected. Now return to the program and change the actual parameters so that it produces different results.

Exercise 12.3. Methods that return a value

The previous examples of methods had a void return type. They were run just to perform a task. Methods can also return a single value. The type of the value returned (**int**, **double**, or **char**) is specified at the beginning of the method heading. When the method is ready to return a value to its caller, the method executes a return statement anywhere in its set of statements. The caller can then use this value in any expression.

To see how a method can return a value, open the file **Example8.java** from the **File** menu. You will see a method called **square**, which expects a double as its parameter, and returns a double representing the square of the parameter. Run the program with several inputs. Then add a new method called **cube** that returns the cube of its parameter. Display the cube of the input value along with its square in the output.

Exercise 12.4. The greatest common divisor

Design, implement, and test a Java method that expects two **int** parameters and returns their greatest common divisor. Be sure to write a pseudocode algorithm first; and be sure to test the program with different pairs of numbers.

Exercise 12.5. Arrays

Recall the algorithms for searching through and sorting lists of data in Chapters 2 and 3 of the text. We can represent a list of numbers conveniently as a data structure called an *array* in Java. An array is just a collection of data values of the same type, where each value is accessible by means of a number called an *index*. For example, if we want to look up the value at the first position in an array **a**, we use the notation **a[0]** in Java. The last value in an array of size *n* would be **a[n - 1]**. We can also store a value in an array at the *i*th position by assigning the value to **a[i - 1]**. To see how arrays are defined as data structures and then manipulated, open the file **Example9.java** from the **File** menu. You will see a constant, **MAX,** that specifies the size or upper bound of the array. Next you will see an array variable declaration. Finally, you will see two loops: one that gets values from the user and inserts them into the array, and the other that looks the values up in the array to display them. Compile and run the program with some test data.

Exercise 12.6. Changing the size of an array

Modify the previous program so that the array can contain five numbers. Test the program until it behaves as expected.

Exercise 12.7. Methods for arrays

Input and output of the contents of an array are such frequently used operations that they ought to be packaged as methods. Define two methods that do just that. They should be *general*; that is, they should work for *any* array of integers. The heading of the array output method should have the form

```
void <method name> (<element type> <array formal parameter name>[ ],
     int length)
```

where the parameter **length** represents the number of data elements in the array. The heading of the array input method should have the form

```
void <method name> (<element type> <array formal parameter name>[ ],
     int &length)
```

where the parameter **length** represents the size of the array before the data are input, and the number of data values actually entered after input.

Test your methods until they behave as expected.

Exercise 12.8. Search for a value

Define a method that searches an array for a value. It should take the target value and the array as input parameters. If the value is found, the method returns its index position; otherwise, the method returns – 1. You can use the algorithm from Chapter 2 if you like. Test your method by passing values into it, asking the user for a target value, running a search, and displaying the appropriate message about the outcome of the search.

Exercise 12.9. Input and output parameters

In Exercise 12.2, you observed a method whose parameter is passed to it for its use. The method has no need to change the value passed to it, nor does the user of the method wish that value to be changed. Therefore, we can say that we pass the value to the method as an *input parameter*. However, there are many cases where we might want the method to do some work on some data passed to it, and return more than one result. Unfortunately, we cannot return these results via parameters that are of type **int**, **double**, or **char**. However, it is possible to change the values of data within an array parameter. To see how this might work, open the file **Example9.java** from the **File** menu. You will see a method **swap** that takes an array parameter and two **int** parameters. The two integers represent positions in the array of data that should be exchanged. This method would thus be useful in situations such as sorting where pairs of data items in an array are swapped. Compile and run the program with different test data.

Exercise 12.10. Sorting an array

Pick your favorite data cleanup or sorting algorithm from Chapter 3 and implement it as a Java method. Test your method in a short tester program.

Worksheet
Lab Experience 12
Java Programming – Methods and Arrays

Name: _____

Course: _____

Exercise 12.1. Methods as abstraction mechanisms

Exercise 12.2. Generalizing methods with parameters

Exercise 12.3. Methods that return a value

Exercise 12.4. The greatest common divisor

Exercise 12.7. Methods for arrays

Exercise 12.8. Search for a value

Exercise 12.10. Sorting an array

Lab Experience 13

Java Programming - Graphics

Objectives

In the previous two lab experiences, you learned the features of a subset of Java. One major drawback of this subset is that programs can interact with users only by displaying text on a terminal screen and taking text as input from the keyboard. More sophisticated programs support the display of graphical images and allow the user to signal inputs by aiming and clicking a mouse at certain spots on the screen. In the next lab experience, you will learn to use a set of graphics methods that allow you to display images and interact with a mouse.

Background

As discussed in Chapter 7 of the text, modern computers represent all output graphically, in a two-dimensional bitmap. Each pixel in this bitmap is located by specifying a point in a window's coordinate system. The origin of this coordinate system (0, 0) lies in the upper left corner of the window. The x and y coordinates increase as we move to the left and to the bottom of the window, respectively.

Graphics programs use a window called a *frame*. A frame has a *graphics object* to which drawing commands are sent. The examples in this lab do the following things:

- Define a frame class
- Create an instance of this class in the **main** method.
- Set the size of the frame and display it.
- Access the frame's graphics object and draw images on it.
- Respond to mouse events, such as pressing the mouse button

The programs discussed in this lab use a class called **LabFrame**, which is provided in the file **LabFrame.class** in the **Examples** folder. The main application class of each program extends the **LabFrame** class, and thus acquires the ability to quit the program (pretty important!) and respond to mouse events easily. In addition, each program in this lab imports the package **java.awt**, which defines classes for performing graphics operations.

There are two ways to access a frame's graphics object. First, one can run the method **getGraphics** to obtain the graphics object. The following code segment does this and draws a line:

```
Graphics g = getGraphics();            // Draw a diagonal line with the
g.drawLine(100, 100, 200, 200);        // end points (100,100) and (200, 200)
```

117

A second way is to define a **paint** method. The following short program does this. Its structure is similar to several of the example programs used in this lab:

```
import java.awt.*;

public class FirstProgram extends LabFrame{

    public void paint(Graphics g){
        g.drawLine(100, 100, 200, 200);        // Draw a diagonal line with the
    }                                          // end points (100,100) and (200, 200)

    public static void main(String[] args){
        LabFrame f = new FirstProgram();
        f.setSize(300, 300);
        f.setVisible(true);
    }
}
```

The computer runs the **paint** method when the frame is displayed and whenever it needs to be refreshed (after resizing, minimizing, etc.). Note that **paint** takes the frame's graphics object as a parameter and sends it a message to draw a line.

Table 13.1 lists some of the methods defined in the **Graphics** class. For other methods, see the documentation for the **Graphics** class on Sun's Web site.

Method	What it does
void setColor(Color color)	Set's the drawing color to the specified color (see Table 13.3 for the color values).
void drawLine(int x1, int y1, int x2, y2)	Draws a line with the specified end points.
void drawOval(int left, int top, int width, int height)	Draws an oval whose bounding rectangle has the specified upper left corner point, width, and height.
void drawRect(int left, int top, int width, int height)	Draws a rectangle with the specified corner point, width, and height.
void drawString(String s, int x, int y)	Draws the string s. The point (x, y) is at the baseline of the first character in the string.

Table 13.1 Some Graphics methods

Table 13.2 lists some of the methods that the **LabFrame** class understands.

Method	What it does
int getWidth()	Returns the current width of the window.
int getHeight()	Returns the current height of the window.
Graphics getGraphics()	Returns the window's graphics object.
void mousePressed(int x, int y)	x and y are the coordinates of the last mouse press.

Method	What it does
`void paint(Graphics g)`	Called when the window needs to be refreshed. `g` is the window's graphics object.
`void repaint()`	Clears the window and calls `paint` to refresh it.
`void setBackground(Color color)`	Sets the color of the window to the specified color (see Table 13.3 for the color values).
`void setSize(int width, int height)`	Sets the width and height of the window to the specified numbers of pixels.
`void setVisible(boolean on)`	Displays the window if `on` is `true` or hide it if `on` is `false`.

Table 13.2 Some `LabFrame` methods

Finally, Table 13.3 lists some color values to use with the **setColor** and **setBackground** methods.

Value	Color
`Color.red`	red
`Color.yellow`	yellow
`Color.blue`	blue
`Color.orange`	orange
`Color.pink`	pink
`Color.cyan`	cyan
`Color.magenta`	magenta
`Color.black`	black
`Color.white`	white
`Color.gray`	gray
`Color.lightGray`	light gray
`Color.darkGray`	dark gray

Table 13.3 Some `Color` values

Exercise 13.1. Put on a happy face

Open the file **Graphic1.java** from the Java compiler's **File** menu. This program draws a simple face. The face consists of a large circle positioned at the center of the window and two smaller circles representing the eyes. Note how the methods **getWidth** and **getHeight** are used to determine the center and radius of the circle. Compile and run the program.

Now return to the editor and modify the program so that the face has nose and a mouth. A simple horizontal line will do for the mouth, although you should be able to add other lines that make the mouth curl up in a smile.

Exercise 13.2. Draw a rectangle interactively

The file **Graphic2.java** contains a program that illustrates the use of drawing and background colors, mouse events, and the method **repaint**. Study the program code first to understand what it does. Then compile and run it. Why does the program allow the user to draw rectangles at different positions? What happens to the previously drawn rectangle when the user draws a new one? Modify the program to draw in different drawing and background colors.

Exercise 13.3. Using `getGraphics` to draw several rectangles

The program in **Graphic2.java** allows the user to draw just one rectangle at a time. Modify the program so that it allows the user to draw several rectangles, by making the following changes to the **mousePressed** method:

- Insert the line **Graphics g = getGraphics**; just above the line **repaint();**
- Copy the four lines of code from the paint method to the line between these two lines.
- Place a comment marker (`//`) in front of the line **repaint();**

Compile and test the program to make sure that it performs just as it did in Exercise 13.2, except that you can draw many rectangles. Explain why your changes to the code produced this result.

Exercise 13.4. Draw the coordinates

Open the file **Graphic3.java** from the **File** menu. When the user presses the mouse button, this program displays the coordinates of the mouse. Compile and run the program. Click the mouse in several positions and note the results. Expand the window by dragging the lower right corner and note that the program still behaves correctly.

Now modify the program so that it displays the coordinates within an oval.

Exercise 13.5. Animation

One way to animate an image is to repeatedly draw it, erase it, adjust its coordinates, and redraw it. The file **Graphic4.java** contains a program that moves a circle across the middle of the window. Compile and run this program.

Now modify the program so that it "bounces" the circle off the right edge of the window and returns it to the left edge.

Exercise 13.6. Defining a graphics method

The file **Graphic5.java** contains a method, **drawFace**, to draw the face displayed in the first program of this lab. The program prompts the user to click the mouse three times. When the user clicks the mouse, the program passes the coordinates as parameters to the method, which draws the circle at these coordinates. Compile and run the program.

Now modify the program by defining a new method, **drawHouse**, to draw a house. A simple triangle atop a rectangle will do. The method should take as parameters the x and y coordinates of the peak of the house's roof. After the user clicks the mouse, the program should draw the face as before, and also draw the house 50 points to the right of the face.

Exercise 13.7. A fractal image

A fractal is a mathematical object that exhibits a repetitive pattern when visualized. A c-curve is a simple kind of fractal that is constructed as follows:

1. A level 0 c-curve is a line segment.
2. A level 1 c-curve consists of a line segment divided in two and bent at right angles. Each of these shorter line segments is actually a level 0 c-curve.

3. A level n c-curve consists of two level $n - 1$ c-curves constructed in this way.

This definition of the c-curve is called a *recursive definition*. A recursive definition consists of one or more simple cases (in this example, a level 0 c-curve is a line segment) and one or more recursive cases (a level n c-curve consists of two level $n - 1$ c-curves). A recursive definition in part defines a thing in terms of itself.

Recursive definitions can be translated to recursive methods in a programming language. Recursive methods have

1. a simple case, in which a task is performed directly, and
2. a recursive case, in which a task is performed by calling the same method again.

The file **Graphic6.java** contains a recursive method, **cCurve**, for drawing c-curves. When the level of the c-curve becomes zero, the method draws a simple line segment and quits. Otherwise, the method draws two c-curves of level $n - 1$. Compile and run this program. It should draw a level 0 c-curve. Now test the program with levels 1, 2, 4, 8, and 12 (you will have to return to the editor after each test to modify the parameter passed as the level).

How many calls of the **cCurve** method are made during the drawing of a level 12 c-curve?

Worksheet
Lab Experience 13
Java Programming – Graphics

Name: _____

Course: _____

Exercise 13.1. Put on a happy face

Exercise 13.2. Draw a rectangle interactively

Exercise 13.4. Draw the coordinates

Exercise 13.5. Animation

Exercise 13.6. Defining a graphics method

Exercise 13.7. A fractal image

Lab Experience 14

LISP Programming

Objectives

The purpose of this lab experience is to introduce you to programming in LISP. You will become acquainted with a LISP programming environment and some of the features of the language. You will see that a LISP programming environment and the LISP language insert yet another layer of virtual machine between the programmer and the computer. In the process, you will come to discover the ways in which a LISP programmer can solve problems at a higher level of abstraction than a C++ programmer.

Background

In Chapter 7 of the text, you were introduced to some of the features of a high-level programming language, C++. You learned that C++ supports the direct coding of the major control structures of pseudo-code algorithms: sequencing, selection, and iteration. C++ also supports the abstraction mechanisms of functions and arrays. In each case, the C++ language allows programmers to express their solutions in terms of standard control and data abstractions, without worrying about how these are implemented on a real machine.

Nevertheless, there are several respects in which the use of C++ does not insulate programmers from machine details as much as they might like. In each of these areas, LISP provides features that sharpen the abstraction barrier between the programmer and the machine.

Memory management

C++ relieves the programmer of many, but not all, of the details of moving data around in memory. For example, evaluating the expression $2 + x$ in assembly language requires a **load** and a **store** operation as well as an **add** operation. The C++ expression specifies just the addition, with no (apparent) data movement. However, the values of expressions in C++ programs are usually stored in variables with the assignment statement, for example, $y = 2 + x$. Indeed, a very large percentage of statements in C++ programs are assignment statements, whose sole purpose is to move data from one place in memory to another. Thus, much of the work of a C++ programmer still involves managing memory.

LISP provides an assignment statement, but its use is not necessary, and good LISP programming practice minimizes it. Good LISP programs consist of combinations of expressions. Data movement occurs only in the underlying virtual machine, where it is completely invisible to the programmer.

Control abstraction

One reason that the assignment statement is so prevalent in C++ programs is that it is used to control iteration. For example, just before a **while** statement, the programmer must initialize a control variable with an assignment statement. Then one must increment or decrement the control variable within the loop, in either case with an assignment statement.

LISP also provides a loop statement, but again, its use is not necessary, and good LISP programming practice minimizes it. Iteration in good LISP programs is implemented by *recursive functions*.

Procedural abstraction

C++ allows programmers to capture common patterns of instructions in functions, whose parameters specialize the patterns for different data. However, C++ does not support very well the *combination* of these patterns into more general or higher-order patterns. For example, one might want to write a function that applies another function to each item in a list of data and returns a list of the results. Or one might want to write a function that takes two other functions as parameters and returns a composite function as the result. The first problem is quite difficult to solve in C++; the second problem is impossible to solve in C++.

LISP functions generalize C++ functions. LISP functions treat any LISP objects--numbers, lists, and even other functions--as *first class data*. That is, any LISP object, including a function, can be passed as a parameter to a LISP function and returned as its value. This feature makes the creation of higher-order functions a virtual requirement of good LISP programming practice.

Data abstraction

C++ provides several built-in data structures, such as arrays. C++ also supports the combination of built-in data structures to form new data structures. However, the built-in data structures are very limited. If programmers wish to use a data structure whose size can grow or shrink at run-time and whose component elements can be of different types, they must write all of the primitive operations on this structure themselves.

The primary built-in data structure in LISP is the list. LISP provides many useful operators for adding data of any type to lists, accessing data in lists, and performing high-order tasks, such as mapping, on lists. In addition, since LISP lists look exactly like LISP expressions or programs, the programmer can explicitly 'store' a program in a data structure and execute it on demand.

Category of virtual machine

The built-in data, operators, and control structures of C++ provide the programmer with a model of a high-level von Neumann machine, but a von Neumann machine nonetheless. The primary characteristics of this model are sequential execution of instructions, branching to other areas of program memory, and movement of data within memory.

LISP provides the programmer with a very different model of a virtual machine. This model, whose primary characteristic is the combination of expressions and recursive functions, is called the *recursive lambda calculus*. Not only does this model yield more natural solutions to a wide range of problems in different domains, but the solutions themselves are much more susceptible to rigorous mathematical analysis for correctness and efficiency. In addition to the 'standard' LISP virtual machine, LISP provides access to other virtual machines in two directions. First, a small set of primitives such as an assignment statement serve as 'hooks' to the underlying von Neumann machine. Second, LISP allows the programmer to construct interpreters for 'metalanguages' that represent other models of virtual machines that you studied Chapter 8 of the text, such as automated theorem-proving and objects with message-passing.

Programming environment

C++ is definitely a higher-level language than assembly language. However, C++ programmers go through much the same process as assembly language programmers to construct, translate, and test their programs. They all must deal with a *batch processing* system; they use a text editor, then a compiler, and finally a run-time system to finish a program.

LISP programs are constructed and run in the same, interactive environment. This environment, known as an *interpreter*, gives programmers instant feedback on the effectiveness of their solutions, and allows them to develop large systems incrementally.

The following exercises will introduce you to the features of LISP enumerated above. You should begin by running your local LISP interpreter. The examples shown here are written in a dialect of LISP called Scheme. You may have to change some syntax if you are using a more traditional LISP. A free Scheme interpreter can be downloaded from http://www.cs.rice.edu/CS/PLT.

Exercise 14.1. Composing expressions

The simplest expressions in LISP are called *atoms*. Type each of the following atoms at the interpreter's prompt, and note the values returned:

```
3

3.14

"Hi there"
```

```
#\a

+

abs
```

Now type each of the following *compound expressions* at the interpreter's prompt, and note the values returned (be sure to place spaces between the numbers and operators):

```
(+ 3 2)

(* 5 (+ 3 2))

(* 3.14 (* 3 3))

(abs (- 1 3))
```

Exercise 14.2. Defining and using functions

LISP lets us define functions quite easily. They can then be used just like the built-in functions **+** and **abs** that you saw in the first exercise. Define a function **square** by typing the following expression at the interpreter's prompt:

```
(define (square x)
  (* x x))
```

Then test it by typing these expressions at the prompt:

```
(square 3)

(+ (square 3) (square 4))

(square (square 3))
```

Exercise 14.3. Defining and using predicates or boolean expressions

A *predicate* is a function that tests a value for a property, returns true if the value satisfies that property, and false otherwise. Type the following atoms, representing true and false, at the interpreter's prompt:

```
#t

#f
```

Now type the following expressions and note the values returned:

```
(= 2 3)
```

```
(= 2 2)

(zero? 0)

(odd? 1)

(atom? "Hi there")

(number? "Hi there")

(not (zero? 1))

(and (>= 2 1) (<= 2 10))
```

Suppose we wanted a new predicate, **in-range?**, that takes three integer parameters and determines whether or not the first integer lies between the other two. Type the following definition of this predicate at the prompt:

```
(define (in-range? number low high)
   (and (>= number low) (<= number high)))
```

Now test it with several numbers to verify that it works correctly.

Exercise 14.4. Making choices with the conditional expression

LISP provides a control structure called the *conditional expression* that works like an **if** statement in C++. It tests a condition, and runs either a consequent expression or an alternative expression, depending on the truth value of the condition. The entire conditional expression then returns the value of the consequent or the alternative expression.

Type the following conditional expression at the interpreter's prompt:

```
(if (> 4 3)
    4
    3)
```

Now we'll define a function that solves a general problem, finding the maximum of two numbers, using the conditional expression:

```
(define (maximum x y)
   (if (> x y)
       x
       y))
```

Test this function with several pairs of numbers.

Exercise 14.5. Iterating with recursion

Consider the problem of computing the factorial of a number, say, 4. The factorial of 4 would be 4 * 3 * 2 * 1 = 24. In general, the factorial of any positive number, n, is n * (n - 1) * (n - 2) * ... * 1. In C++, we could solve this problem with a **while** loop:

```
factorial = 1;
while (n > 0)
{
    factorial = factorial * n;
    n = n - 1;
}
```

However, there is a much simpler *recursive* definition of the factorial of a number. It consists of two cases:

```
n! = 1, when n = 0.
n! = n * (n - 1)!, when n > 0.
```

These two cases translate directly to a LISP function that uses a conditional expression and a *recursive call*, rather than a loop:

```
(define (factorial n)
   (if (zero? n)
       1
       (* n (factorial (- n 1))))))
```

Test this function with several numbers. If your interpreter has a trace feature, turn it on with **(trace factorial)** and run the function again with several numbers.

The greatest common divisor of two integers is the largest integer by which both are evenly divisible. You saw an iterative version of Euclid's method for computing this value in Chapter 8, Exercise 1. The method is defined recursively as follows:

```
gcd(a, b) = a, when b = 0.
gcd(a, b) = gcd(b, remainder of dividing a by b), when b > 0.
```

Using the **remainder** function, the conditional expression, and a recursive call, define and test a LISP function that computes the greatest common divisor of two integers.

Exercise 14.6. Using symbols and quotation

LISP was originally designed for processing the lists of symbols used in algebraic expressions. A *symbol* in LISP is a special kind of atom. You have seen some symbols in previous exercises, such as **abs**, **square**, and **+**. These symbols also serve as names of LISP functions: you can verify that by typing them at the interpreter's prompt to see what happens. Other symbols, such as **ken** and **tom**, may not be the names of LISP objects at all: if you type them at the prompt, you might get an error message. These symbols may mean something to us, however, and we would like the interpreter to treat them just as symbols. To do this, we prefix the symbol with a single quote mark (**'**). The quote mark informs the interpreter that it should return just the thing quoted; indeed, you may quote any LISP expression to achieve this effect. Type out the following quoted expressions at the prompt:

```
'ken

'tom

'abs

'(ken and tom are the authors of this manual)

'(+ 3 4)
```

Note that some of the expressions look like LISP programs that should return numbers, but they do not. Now try typing each expression without the quote mark and note the difference in the results.

Exercise 14.7. Constructing and accessing lists

The list is the basic data structure in LISP. A list looks just like a compound expression. Lists can be of arbitrary size, and they can contain any LISP data objects. For example, the list (ken and tom are the authors of this manual) contains nine symbols, while the list **(+ 3 4)** contains one symbol and two integers. The interpreter takes a compound expression to be a list if it is quoted; otherwise, it takes the expression to be the application of a function to its parameters. Thus, one way to construct a list is simply to quote it at the prompt. Another way is to use the function **list**. For example, the list (ken and tom are the authors of this manual) could be constructed by typing

```
(list 'ken 'and 'tom 'are 'the 'authors 'of 'this 'manual)
```

You should verify that this is the case now. Then try

```
(list ken and tom are the authors)
```

The most primitive list constructor is the function **cons**. To construct a list of one element, you apply **cons** to the element and the empty list, represented as a quoted pair of empty parentheses:

```
(cons 'ken '())

(cons 2 '())

(cons + '())
```

To construct a list of two or more elements, more **cons**es are required:

```
(cons 'ken (cons 'tom '()))

(cons '+ (cons 3 (cons 4 '())))
```

Once you have a list, you can access two parts: the first element in it, and a list containing the rest of the elements in the list after the first one. The function **car** returns the first element, while the function **cdr** returns the list of the remaining elements. Type the following expressions at the prompt to see this:

```
(car '(tom and ken))

(cdr '(tom and ken))

(car (cdr '(tom and ken)))

(cdr (cdr (cdr '(tom and ken))))
```

Exercise 14.8. Recursive list processing

Suppose we wanted to determine the length of a list. It turns out that **length** is a built-in function that we can already use for this purpose. For example the expression (length '(hello there)) should return 2. Now suppose that we had to define this function ourselves. One way to do this is to define the length of a list recursively:

```
length(list) = 0, when list is empty.
length(list) = 1 +
       length(the rest of the list after the first element), otherwise.
```

All we need is a predicate to test the list to see if it's empty. The built-in predicate **null?** does this. If the list is not empty, we add one to the length of the rest of the list after the first element, by calling our function recursively with the **cdr** of the list as its parameter:

```
(define (our-length lyst)
  (if (null? lyst)
      0
      (+ 1 (our-length (cdr lyst)))))
```

Put a trace on this function if your system supports it, and run the function with lists of various lengths.

Exercise 14.9. Defining and using higher-order functions

Suppose we wanted to compute the summation of a series of integers between a lower and an upper bound. Here is a recursive definition of a summation:

```
sum(low, high) = 0, when low > high.
sum(low, high) = low + sum(low + 1, high), otherwise.
```

The corresponding recursive function in LISP is quite easily defined:

```
(define (sum low high)
  (if (> low high)
      0
      (+ low (sum (+ low 1) high))))
```

Run this function with several pairs of numbers and a tracer on, if possible.

Now suppose we want to take the summation of the squares of all the integers in a series. We could write another function that does just what **sum** does, but it adds the square of **low** to the sum of the rest of the series:

```
(define (sum low high)
  (if (> low high)
      0
      (+ (square low) (sum (+ low 1) high))))
```

In fact, there may be numerous functions like square that we wish to apply during summations. Instead of writing a separate summation function for each special case, we would like to capture the general pattern of summations in one function and parameterize it for the special functions we wish to apply. All we need to do is add a parameter for the special function to our original function:

```
(define (sum low high proc)
  (if (> low high)
      0
      (+ (proc low) (sum (+ low 1) high proc))))
```

Instead of **square**, we see **proc**, which can be any function whose parameter is an integer and whose return value is also an integer. Now you can run the new version of sum with the **square** function you defined earlier, for example:

```
(sum 1 5 square)
```

Worksheet
Lab Experience 14
LISP Programming

Name: _____

Course: _____

Exercise 14.1. Composing expressions

Write the values:

```
(+ 3 2)

(* 5 (+ 3 2))

(* 3.14 (* 3 3))

(abs (- 1 3))
```

Exercise 14.2. Defining and using functions

Write the values:

```
(square 3)

(+ (square 3) (square 4))

(square (square 3))
```

Exercise 14.3. Defining and using predicates or boolean expressions

Write the values:

```
(= 2 3)

(= 2 2)

(zero? 0)

(odd? 1)

(atom? "Hi there")

(number? "Hi there")

(not (zero? 1))

(and (>= 2 1) (<= 2 10))
```

Exercise 14.4. Making choices with the conditional expression

Write the value:

```
(if (> 4 3)
    4
    3)
```

Exercise 14.5. Iterating with recursion

Write your definition of the **gcd** function in Scheme:

Exercise 14.7. Constructing and accessing lists

Write the values:

```
(cons 'ken '())

(cons 2 '())

(cons + '())

(cons 'ken (cons 'tom '()))

(cons '+ (cons 3 (cons 4 '())))

(car '(tom and ken))

(cdr '(tom and ken))

(car (cdr '(tom and ken)))

(cdr (cdr (cdr '(tom and ken))))
```

Lab Experience 15

Programming Language Translation

Objectives

In previous lab experiences, you observed programs in three very different programming languages. You began with a language whose form maps directly to the physical structure of a real computer. You expressed instructions and data in terms of strings of 1s and 0s in this language. The computer easily understood what these strings meant, but you probably had to go through a painful process of translation to figure out what you were saying in machine language. Then you learned to use a language that still reflects the structure of the computer, but employs terms that are closer to those you would use if you were describing the instructions and data to another person. This language requires a program called an assembler to translate programs to machine language. Finally, you learned to use a language whose sentences more closely resemble those you would use in English to describe the solution of a problem. This language, Java, requires a program called a compiler to translate your sentences into machine language.

The main point of these lab exercises was not only to show you that there are different languages for expressing programs. The languages you used also represent layers of virtual machine bridging the gap between the structure of a real computer and the structure of your thoughts. It is no exaggeration to say that if this gap had not been bridged, most of the interesting and useful software that we have would not exist.

The disciplines of programming language design and translation are concerned with constructing languages and translators that help to close the conceptual gap between computers and human beings. The purpose of the present lab experience is to expose you to the translation process for converting one virtual machine into another. The following lab exercises will allow you to explore what happens when a program translates code in one language into code in another language. First you will examine how an assembler translates an assembly language program to a machine language program. Then you will study the process by which a Java compiler can translate a Java program to an assembly language program.

One note of clarification is in order before we begin this lab. We said that a Java compiler "can" translate Java programs to assembly language programs, but most Java compilers actually translate Java programs to programs whose code is called *byte code*. Byte code programs are then executed by a *byte code interpreter*, sometimes also called a ***Java virtual machine*** (JVM). A byte code interpreter works something like the LISP interpreter mentioned in Lab 14, except that the Java programmer never sees the byte code. However, for the purposes of the current lab, we use a Java compiler for a very small subset of Java that does translate Java programs to assembly language programs.

For exercises 15.1-15.4, select the **Assembler** from the main menu.

Exercise 15.1 Syntax analysis

Open the file **Example1.asm** from the **File** menu of the assembler. You should see the assembly language program for adding two numbers in the source pane. Select **Assemble** from the **Assmbler** menu. You should see a program listing appear in the listing pane, with no syntax errors reported. Before a program can be translated, the translator must verify that there are no syntax errors in the source program. Now go back to the source pane and edit the program by changing `.begin` to `begin` (just delete the period from that line). Run the assembler again and watch what happens. Do you see where the error occurred, and was the message about it informative? Now put the period back in front of `begin` and edit the source program again, by deleting the `t` from `halt`. What kind of message do you suppose you will see this time? Why do you think that the assembler bothers to signal that there are syntax errors and to require that programs be syntactically correct before allowing the process to continue?

Exercise 15.2 Static semantic analysis

Reload the example assembly language program, and edit it by replacing `add y` with `add a`. Assemble the program and think about the error message. Suppose that the assembler ignored errors of this sort. What do you think would happen when the computer tries to execute the instruction `add a`? Now reload the program, and insert the instruction `jump q` right after `.begin`. Assemble the program and explain the error. Insert a label for `q` before `halt` and reassemble. Then insert the label `k` before `add y` and reassemble. What are the rules governing instruction labels in assembly language, and how are they different from variable labels? Now reload the program, and change the number 4 to 400000 and reassemble. What sort of error is this, and why is it important to detect it?

Exercise 15.3 Object code

Reload the example assembly language program, assemble it, and select **View Object Code** from the **Assembler** menu. Is there a one-to-one correspondence between each assembly language instruction or datum and each machine code instruction or datum? Is there a direct mapping between the sentences of assembly language and the sentences of machine language? Verify from the table of opcodes in Lab Experience 9 that this is so. Now pick **Execute** from the **Assembler** menu. Step through the execution of the program by the machine language interpreter. Try to describe how machine language and assembly language are similar. Try to describe what is involved in translating a single assembly language instruction to a machine code instruction (picking an instruction from the example program will help).

Exercise 15.4 Symbol table

Return to the assembler from the machine language interpreter, and pick **View Symbol Table** from the **Assembler** menu. Verify that the address of each data label is correct. Why are there no instruction labels in the table? Add an instruction label to the source program, reassemble, and view the symbol table once more. Is the address of the instruction label correct? How do you suppose that the assembler uses the symbol table to detect errors in the source program?

For the following exercises, select the **Language Translation** from the main menu. Then select **Java** from the **Language** menu.

15.5 Syntax analysis

Open the program **Example1.java** from the **File** menu. You should see a Java program displaying the sum of two numbers in the source pane. Pick **Compile** from the **Translator** menu. This is the only Java program in the Examples folder that compiles correctly in this lab. The reason for this is that the subset of Java used for this lab is much smaller than the one used in labs 11-13. In particular, the present version of Java lacks the data types **double**, **char**, string, and array, the operators *****, **/**, and **%**, and you cannot define methods. The reason for this is that these features do not translate to features supported by our assembly language.

Now try introducing the following syntax errors into the program, making sure that you reload the program from the file for each experiment:

a. Delete the word **main**, and compile.

b. Delete the first **{**, and compile.

c. Delete the first assignment operator (**=**), and compile.

d. Delete the addition operator (**+**), and compile.

How informative are the syntax error messages of this compiler, as compared with those generated by the assembler? Why is the compiler so fussy about Java's syntax?

Exercise 15.6 Static semantic analysis

Change the word **sum** to the word **result** in the list of variables declared at the top of the program, and compile it. What information do the error messages provide? Why do you suppose that Java identifiers must be declared before they are used in statements? Now change the number 2 to a huge number, such as 4000000. Compile the program and explain why it is useful that the compiler catches this error before the program is translated and executed.

Exercise 15.7 Object code

Reload and compile the example program. Select **View Object Code** from the **Translator** menu. You should see the equivalent program in assembly language in the Object Code pane (Figure 15.1).

```
Java Translator - Example1.java
File  Translator  Language

// Example1.java                          .begin
                                          load first
public class Example1{                    add second
                                          store sum
   public static void main(String[] args){  out sum
      final int first = 4;                 halt
      final int second = 5;               second: .data 5
      int sum;                            first: .data 4
      sum = first + second;               sum: .data 0
      System.out.println(sum);            .end
   }


}
```

Figure 15.1 The object code of a Java program

Look at the data declaration part of the assembly language program, and compare that with the data declarations in the Java program. Note that there is a correspondence between the Java data names and the data labels in the assembly language program. Try to explain the purpose of the other data label in the assembly language program. It will help to scan back up to the assembly language instructions to see how this other data label is used. How many assembly language instructions, on the average, are required to implement a Java statement? Which Java statements are the easiest to translate, and which ones seem to be the most difficult? If you are still stumped on the need for a separate data label for output, edit the Java program so that it outputs the sum of the two numbers without using the variable **sum**. Compile and view the object code once more.

Exercise 15.8 Translating a Java loop

Edit the program so that it displays all of the numbers between the first number and the second number. Compile the program and view the object code. You should see an equivalent loop in assembly language.

Exercise 15.9 Code optimization

Examine the translation of the Java assignment statement **first = first + 1** in the assembly language program. How many instructions does this simple Java statement require? Explain how the compiler could have translated this Java assignment statement to one assembly language instruction (*Hint*:

change the Java statement to **++first** and recompile). Explain how the translated program would run more efficiently if the compiler as a rule translated such statements this new way.

Exercise 15.10 Symbol table

Pick **View Symbol Table** from the **Translator** menu. Note that there are two tables, one for symbolic labels and one for literal labels. Explain the difference between these two kinds of label. Explain the difference between a Java constant and a Java variable. Try putting a Java constant on the left side of an assignment statement in the Java program, and compile the program and explain the error message. How do you suppose that the compiler uses the symbol table to translate the Java program to an assembly language program? Explain the differences between a Java compiler's symbol table and an assembler's symbol table.

Worksheet
Lab Experience 15
Programming language Translation

Name: _____

Course: _____

Exercise 15.1 Syntax analysis

Exercise 15.2 Static semantic analysis

Exercise 15.3 Object code

Exercise 15.4 Symbol table

15.5 Syntax analysis

a. Delete the word **main**, and compile.

b. Delete the first **{**, and compile.

c. Delete the first assignment operator (**=**), and compile.

d. Delete the addition operator (**+**), and compile.

Exercise 15.6 Static semantic analysis

Exercise 15.7　Object code

Exercise 15.9　Code optimization

Exercise 15.10 Symbol table

Lab Experience 16

Turing Machines

Objectives

In this laboratory session, you will learn to use a Turing machine simulator that is included as one of the modules in the lab software package. The simulator allows you to enter the specifications for a Turing machine and its tape and then observe the execution of the machine on the given tape. This can be done in either a step or run mode. In this lab, you will test some of the examples from the text and try out minor modifications to these. Then in the next laboratory session, you will be able to design and test your own solutions to some new Turing machine exercises.

Background

To get into the Turing machine simulator, click on the **Turing Machine** button of the main button menu of the lab software package. You should now have a window like that shown in Figure 16.1. Briefly, what you see is a window divided into five panes. The **Command** pane contains a set of buttons that you will use to control the simulation once the states, instructions and tape input have been entered into the simulator. The **Tape** pane is a vertical representation of the tape with up corresponding to left in the text and down corresponding to right. The darkened cell indicates the current location of the read head. Skipping to the fourth pane, the **State** pane will contain a list of states that have been defined for the machine. A darkened state will indicate the current state of the machine. The third pane will contain the instructions that have been defined for this present state. The labels at the top of the pane are present to remind us that an instruction consists of five components: the current state (labeled CUR), the input character being read by the tape head (labeled INP), the output character to be written on the tape (labeled OUT), the next state to move to (labeled NXT), and the direction to move the tape head (labeled MOV). If it is the case that there is an instruction for the present state and current tape cell, this instruction will be darkened. Thus, at any time, the tape pane should represent the current status of the tape and the location of the read head, the state pane should contain the states with the present state darkened, and the instruction pane contains the instructions for the present state with the instruction that applies to the current situation darkened. The **Description** pane contains a description of the current state. It is important to have a clear statement of the situation modeled by a given state. This will be useful to you in finding the source of errors in your machines - the state description doesn't match the current situation - and will make it possible for others (in particular your instructor) to understand what you had in mind when you designed the machine. Finally, there are three important menus at the top of the screen. The **Tape** menu contains options for manipulating the tape, the **Instructions** menu options control the entry and management of instructions, and the **States** menu does the same for the states. We'll cover the details of these as we work on the exercises.

Figure 16.1 The Turing machine simulator.

Exercise 16.1. Parity checker

In this exercise, you will work with the parity checker Turing machine that was covered in the text. Recall that this machine adds a 1 to the end of the input string if the string contains an even number of 1's and adds a 0 to the end if the string contains an odd number of 1's. In order to ease into the use of the simulator, you will load in a solution of this problem that we provide for you. You will experiment with the machine with different input strings, and then you will make some changes to the machine and test those. So, to get started, open the **example.sta** file from the **File** menu. After the states are loaded into the simulator, the screen should appear as in Figure 16.2. Notice that there are three states. State 1 is now the current state, and it represents the situation in which we have processed an even number of 1's in the input string. There are three instructions having state 1 as the current state, and the one darkened applies to present state 1 with the read head being on a blank cell. The darkened instruction "1b13R" in Figure 16.2 applies if we are in state 1 and the current tape symbol is a blank. The third part of an instruction is the symbol to be written in the current tape cell. So, for the darkened instruction, the blank is to be replaced with a 1. The fourth component indicates the next state we move into; here we go to state 3. The final component indicates the direction to move the read head. So, in words, the instruction "1b13R" says that if we are in state 1, with current symbol blank (b), then we should replace the blank with a 1, move to state 3, and move the read head to the right. We should also mention that only a portion of the tape is shown at any one time. The simulator proceeds as if there is an indefinite number of cells to the left (up) and to the right (down). When necessary, the pane should scroll to show the appropriate cells. To see the instructions and descriptions for the other two states, simply click on the state in the **State** pane. Go ahead and do this now.

Figure 16.2 Parity checker states loaded.

Now to get some initial data on the tape, select the **Load Tape** option from the **Tape** menu. Using the dialog box that appears, find the **Example.tap** file in the **Examples** folder and open it. The machine should now appear as in Figure 16.3. Here we see that the string 110100101 has been loaded onto the tape, the read head is on the first 1, we are currently in state 1, and the instruction that applies, 1112R, would leave a 1 in this cell, would change to state 2, and would move the read head to the right (down). Try executing this instruction by clicking on the **Step** button. This button is used to make the simulator execute a single instruction from the present situation. The machine should now appear as in Figure 16.4.

Figure 16.3 Parity checker tape loaded.

Notice that we have moved into state 2 and that the read head has moved to the second 1 in the string. Now continue to follow the execution of the parity checker by clicking the **Step** button three more times and observe the progress each time. For each of these steps, explain the details of what has happened (Worksheet). When you are clear as to how this is working, click on the **Run** button to let the machine run on its own until it finishes its task. A message will now appear informing you that the simulator has halted. Click on the **OK** button to see the final result after the parity bit has been added to the end of the string. Notice that a 0 has been added to the end of the string since the original string contained an odd number of 1's.

Figure 16.4 Parity checker after first step.

The authors' first attempt at solving the parity check problem contained an error. The machine did fine in terms of putting the correct parity bit at the end of the input string. However, it did not know when to stop and kept moving the head to the right over the blanks. By the way, the simulator will continue to add blank cells to either end as the head moves past the end of the visible cells. So, we had a runaway Turing machine on our hands. In case you get tired of watching a run, click on the **Step** button. Don't forget to reset the current state to the start state, which is always state 1.

Exercise 16.2. Parity checker with other input tapes

Now that you have seen the machine operate on this one input string, you should try it out on some other inputs. Select the **Reset** button before editing the tape. The easiest way to manufacture a new input string (without loading it from an existing tape file) is to use the **Initialize** option under the **Tape** menu. This option will allow you to type in a string of symbols that will be loaded into the tape cells. Other options under the **Tape** menu and its nested **Symbol** menu are the following:

- **New** puts blanks (b's) in all of the tape cells.
- **Save** allows you to save a sample tape string in a tape file for future use.
- **Add** adds a symbol at the left end of the tape string.
- **Delete** removes the current symbol and shifts the read head to the right.
- **Change** to change the symbol in the selected cell.

Use the **Initialize** option now to enter the string 11111. Test the parity checker by running it on this string and the following strings: 000000, 101010101, and 1. For each of these, give the string that results after the simulator has added the parity bit (Worksheet).

Exercise 16.3. Modifying the parity checker

One important method for solving complex problems is to break the given problem into a series of manageable subproblems. If we can solve the subproblems, then a solution of the main problem can be obtained by letting the output of one subproblem become the input to the next subproblem. In the context of Turing machines, we would want the output tape from one machine to be the input to the next machine. Since we have adopted the convention that the read head is originally on the first non-blank cell, we would want to be sure that when a machine completes its task, it puts the read head back on the first non-blank cell. So, let's make the necessary changes to the parity checker in order that the read head is in the proper position when the machine halts.

What changes are necessary? First, once the parity bit is added, we move the head to the left until we come to a blank cell (perhaps out of sight at the top of the tape pane, originally). Then, we move the head one cell to the right. This can all take place in state 3. However, when the head is moved to the right in the end, we need to change to a new halting state. Otherwise, the new instructions of state 3 would cause the head to move back to the left. Notice that the description for state 3 is no longer accurate since the task is not finished until the head is properly placed. Now select the **Reset** button and make the following required changes to the machine:

1. In the state pane, select state 3. Delete the description for state 3. Enter a new description for state 3, something like, "Parity bit added, moving head left to first non-blank cell".

2. Add a new state, state 4, by selecting the **Add** option under the **State** menu. Enter a description, something like "Task completed, read head back in original position".

3. Change the two instructions that actually add the parity bit so that they move the read head to the left rather than to the right. To do this, you must first delete the instruction and then add a new instruction. First, select state 1 in the state pane. Then select the instruction (1,b,1,3,R) in the instruction pane. Choose the **Delete** option under the **Instruction** menu. Now select the **Add** option under this menu. You will be presented with menus for the present symbol (choose b), the next symbol (choose 1), the next state (choose 3), and the tape action (choose L). Now select state 2 and change the instruction (2,b,0,3,R) to (2,b,0,3,L).

4. Add instructions for state 3 that will keep moving the head to the left as long as the input cell is 0 or 1. Select state 3 and add the instructions (3,0,0,3,L) and (3,1,1,3,L).

5. Finally, add an instruction to move the head back to the right and go into state 4 once the read head encounters a blank cell in state 3. Select state 3 and add a new instruction (3,b,b,4,R).

Now test the altered machine on several input tapes. Notice that each time the machine halts now, the tape head is in position for another run; so try putting the state back to state 1 and clicking on the **Run** button. Try this a few times. What always happens to the parity bit after the first run? Why is this? Answer on the Worksheet.

Exercise 16.4. Producing report for modified parity checker

Assuming that things have gone well so far, you are now ready to produce a report for this exercise. To do this, select on the **Save Report** option from the **File** menu. First, you will be prompted for your name. Next, you will be prompted for your course and section number. Enter the appropriate information to identify your lab section as requested by your instructor. When you are prompted for the machine description, give a brief description, something like "Adds a parity bit to the end of a string of 0's and 1's and puts the read head in the original position". The report will include this information along with a listing of the states together with the state descriptions and instructions. At the end of this process, the report will be sent to a file and you can turn it in electronically or print it from a word processor.

Exercise 16.5. Unary adder

Recall that the unary representation of a non-negative integer consists of a string of 1's with one more 1 than the numerical value of the integer. In this exercise, you will enter and test the Turing machine presented in the text to add two unary numbers. So, starting with a clear machine, add the following states and descriptions: State 1 (Erase the leftmost 1), State 2 (Erase the second 1), State 3 (Scan from left to right and replace the blank separating the two numbers with a 1), and State 4 (Task completed - tape contains the sum of the two input numbers). Now select State 1 and add the instruction (1,1,b,2,R), select State 2 and add the instruction (2,1,b,3,R), select State 3 and add the instructions (3,1,1,3,R) and (3,b,1,4,R). Now test the adder with several addition problems. On the Worksheet, the string that is produced when the original tape contains the string 1111b11111.

Worksheet
Lab Experience 16
Turing Machines

Name: _____

Course: _____

Exercise 16.1. Parity checker

Explain in detail what actions take place when the second step is executed:

Explain in detail what actions take place when the third step is executed:

Explain in detail what actions take place when the fourth step is executed:

Exercise 16.2. Parity checker with other input tapes

Resulting string after parity bit is added to 11111:

Resulting string after parity bit is added to 000000:

Resulting string after parity bit is added to 101010101:

Resulting string after parity bit is added to 1:

Exercise 16.3. Modifying the parity checker

What happens when we run the modified parity checker on its own output?

Explain why this always happens:

Exercise 16.5. Unary adder

Give the string produce when the adder is given input string 1111b11111:

Lab Experience 17

Turing Machines

Objectives

In this laboratory, you will continue your work with the Turing machine simulator. This time you are asked to design various Turing machines rather than working with solutions which have been provided for you. In this way you test your ability to create Turing machine solutions to problems, not just your understanding of how a Turing machine works.

Background

While the simulator is designed to allow easy modifications to a machine, it is still much easier to give considerable thought to your solution before entering it into the simulator. It pays to work out descriptions for the states beforehand - if you don't have a clear idea of the role of a state, then there is a good chance that there will be a problem with your solution. Try not to use more states than necessary. One way to know that you need a new state is if you find that you are giving conflicting instructions for the state; i.e., if you are wanting the machine to do two different things from the present state with the same current tape symbol. For example, if you want the machine to replace a 1 with a 0 in some situations, but leave the 1 alone in other situations, these two cases must be modeled by different states. Also, be sure to test your solution with several different input tapes. The fact that the machine works for one input does not mean that it will work for all inputs. It is a good idea to try some rather extreme cases since these are often the cases that cause trouble. For example, if the input is required to be a string of 1's (with at least one 1), then be sure to see what happens if there is just a single 1.

Exercise 17.1. Tape eraser

Design, enter into the simulator, test and produce a report for a Turing machine which assumes the tape head is on the first of a string of non-blank characters. The machine should erase all of these characters until it encounters a blank. Draw a state-transition diagram for the machine on the Worksheet.

Exercise 17.2.   Increase unary number by 2

Design, enter into the simulator, test and produce a report for a Turing machine which assumes the tape head is on the first of a string of 1's. The machine should add two more 1's to the right hand end of this string of 1's. Draw a state-transition diagram for the machine on the Worksheet.

Exercise 17.3.   Bit sorter

Design, enter into the simulator, test and produce a report for a Turing machine which assumes the tape head is on the first of a string of 0's and 1's. The output should be the same number of 0's and the same number of 1's, only with the 0's all appearing before the 1's. For example, if the input were 10011011, then the output should be 00011111. For an algorithm to solve this problem, we suggest you try the following approach: Moving from the left, each time you encounter a 1, replace it with a marker, say an x. Then move to the right to see if there is a 0 to the right of the 1 being processed. If there is, replace the 0 with a 1 and then move back to change the x to a 0. Continue this process until either there are no further 1's or else there are no 0's to the right of a 1. Draw a state-transition diagram for the machine on the Worksheet.

Exercise 17.4.   Reverse image

Design, enter into the simulator, test and produce a report for a Turing machine that makes a copy of its input string only with the bits in reverse order. For example, if the input string is 110101, then the output tape should contain this string followed by a blank that is followed by the reverse string 101011. Draw a state-transition diagram for the machine on the Worksheet.

Exercise 17.5.   Unary subtractor

This is a more challenging exercise. Design, enter into the simulator, test and produce a report for a Turing machine which takes as input two positive integers in unary form, the first of which is larger than the second. The output should be the difference of the two integers, also in unary form. Draw a state-transition diagram for the machine on the Worksheet.

Worksheet
Lab Experience 17
Turing Machines

Name: _____

Course: _____

Exercise 17.1. **Tape eraser**

State-transition diagram:

Exercise 17.2.   Increase unary number by 2

State-transition diagram:

Exercise 17.3.   Bit sorter

State-transition diagram:

Exercise 17.4. Reverse image

State-transition diagram:

Exercise 17.5. Unary subtractor

State-transition diagram:

Lab Experience 18

Spreadsheets

Objectives

In this lab session, you will be introduced to the use of a spreadsheet program. The goal is not to cover all aspects of this extensive tool, but rather to give you the flavor of working with such a program. Most people learn to use sophisticated software packages by first learning how to accomplish a few simple tasks and then gradually increasing their skills as further needs arise. Often this learning is achieved by reading manuals, taking short courses, and asking more experienced users.

Background

Since most lab installations are equipped with spreadsheet programs, we will have you work with a full-blown package rather than a simplified program that we might include with the lab software. This chapter is based on the Microsoft Excel (Office 97) package. If you are working with a different package (as is quite likely), many of the details will be different, but the outcomes should be essentially the same. In this case your instructor should provide you with modifications to the instructions given here.

Included on your lab software diskette is an Excel spreadsheet called **example.xls**. If you are working with Excel, you should now open **example.xls** from Excel's **File** menu. Otherwise, open a new spreadsheet and enter the data as shown in Figure 18.1. The data shown here represent grades for a lab section of fifteen students on each of five lab projects. The exercises will lead you through a set of operations to perform on the spreadsheet. The instructions will be given for Excel - you should modify them to conform to the package you are using.

Figure 18.1 The LabGrades Spreadsheet

Exercise 18.1. Changing format of cells

Spreadsheet packages typically provide extensive capabilities for formatting the data stored in selected cells. With Excel, you can see many possibilities under the Format menu. For example, you can change the text font of the selected cells, center data within the cells, make borders, or make the text bold. There are shortcuts for some of these options. For example, to make the data in a set of selected cells bold, you simply click on the **B** button on the button bar just below the menu bar. In order to make our column headers stand out, you should now select the cells containing these headers by dragging over them. Now click the bold button, and the cells should appear in bold format.

Exercise 18.2. Scores for Lab 6

Now click on cell G1 (column G, row 1). Proceed to type in the Lab 6 column header and the students' scores as shown in Figure 18.2. When you type the data for a cell and press "return", the cell selector should move to the cell below. You can change the width of the cells in Column F, for example, by putting the cursor on the line between the F and the G. Hold the mouse button down and move left or right to change the width.

= AVERAGE(Bx:Bx)
= ROUND(AVERAGE(Bx:Bx),0)

= AVERAGE(Bx:Bx)
= ROUND(AVERAGE(Bx:Bx),0)

	A	B	C	D	E	F	G
1	Name	Lab 1	Lab 2	Lab 3	Lab 4	Lab 5	Lab 6
2	Miller, Bob	88	92	86	80	91	94
3	Bong, Chang	95	87	92	96	89	93
4	Wilson, Mary	84	60	82	78	80	70
5	Pavlovic, Martin	92	86	94	80	82	76
6	Carter, Louis	65	70	75	60	68	77
7	Sokol, Adrian	60	0	50	70	40	0
8	Duncan, Jim	95	98	94	60	88	92
9	Johnson, Carl	86	82	90	92	80	84
10	Artel, Lois	74	66	55	74	70	72
11	Taylor, Charles	86	82	90	85	78	80
12	Roberts, Victoria	98	88	85	84	92	96
13	Alou, Pedro	76	78	70	80	72	82
14	Adams, Ben	86	80	78	74	77	72
15	Beckley, John	66	50	52	54	64	68
16	Smith, Debbie	78	82	75	80	70	72

Figure 18.2 Adding Scores for Lab 6

Exercise 18.3. Student averages

Now click on Cell H1 and type in a column title of Avg. This column will hold the lab averages for the students. Now with cell H2 selected, you will type in a formula for the average of the first student's lab scores. We signify that we are entering a formula by typing the "=" sign. Excel has a built in function called AVERAGE that computes the average over a range of cells. In our case, we can simply type in "=AVERAGE(B2:G2)" to indicate that we want the average of the cells from B2 through G2; i.e., the scores for the student Bob Miller. However, we want the averages to be rounded to the nearest integer; so type "=ROUND(AVERAGE(B2:G2),0)". The 0 indicates that we want no digits to the right of the decimal point in the result. A 1 in this position would cause the result to be rounded to the nearest tenth, etc. When you type the formula, as in Figure 18.3, and hit the "return", the average for the first student should appear in cell H2. Now, to compute the averages for the other students, we need only copy the formula from cell H2 into

Figure 18.3   Formula to Average First Student's Scores

the other cells from H3 through H16. So select cell H2 and choose the "Copy" option from the **edit** menu. Now select cells H2 through H16 by dragging over them, and choose "Paste" from the **edit** menu. Click on H4 and notice how the formula has been adjusted to apply to this row. The sheet should now appear as in Figure 18.4.

$$= IF\ (C12 >= B2,\ ``P",\ ``F")$$

$$= IF\ (B4 <= 7,\ ``Yes",\ ``No")$$

	A	B	C	D	E	F	G	H
1	Name	Lab 1	Lab 2	Lab 3	Lab 4	Lab 5	Lab 6	Avg
2	Miller, Bob	88	92	86	80	91	94	89
3	Bong, Chang	95	87	92	96	89	93	92
4	Wilson, Mary	84	60	82	78	80	70	76
5	Pavlovic, Martin	92	86	94	80	82	76	85
6	Carter, Louis	65	70	75	60	68	77	69
7	Sokol, Adrian	60	0	50	70	40	0	37
8	Duncan, Jim	95	98	94	60	88	92	88
9	Johnson, Carl	86	82	90	92	80	84	86
10	Artel, Lois	74	66	55	74	70	72	69
11	Taylor, Charles	86	82	90	85	78	80	84
12	Roberts, Victoria	98	88	85	84	92	96	91
13	Alou, Pedro	76	78	70	80	72	82	76
14	Adams, Ben	86	80	78	74	77	72	78
15	Beckley, John	66	50	52	54	64	68	59
16	Smith, Debbie	78	82	75	80	70	72	76

Figure 18.4   Averages Computed for all Students

Exercise 18.4. Averages for individual Labs

In row 18, put a row title of "Lab Averages" in cell A18, and enter formulas to have the column averages for the individual labs appear at the bottom. Now, temporarily change one of the lab scores and watch the row and column averages update automatically. For example, go to cell D8, remember the score there, and type 30 and "return". Now put the score back the way it was so that your results will compare with what we show in the figures.

Exercise 18.5. Letter grades

Next, we want column I to contain letter grades for the students. These letter grades will be based on the scores in the Avg column, with 90 and above getting A, 80-89 getting B, 70-79 getting C, 60-69 getting D and below 60 getting F. So, make a column header called "Grade" in cell I1. We could manually enter the letter grades; however, if we had to change a lab grade later, we would have to be sure to make the change, if necessary, in the letter grade. Since we can copy and paste from cell to cell, and from sheet to sheet, if we determine the formula once, we'll be able to use it over and over. To keep things simple for the moment, let's assume that we are using pass/fail grades with 70 as the cutoff point. In cell I2, type the formula "=IF(H2>=70,"P","F")". This says that if the value in H2 is greater than or equal to 70, then the value to be put in I2 is the letter P, and otherwise, the letter F should be the value for I2. Notice that this is the "if-then-else" structure that we have already encountered in pseudocode, hardware circuitry, assembly language programming, and high level programming. So, in effect, we are programming the cell of the spreadsheet with an if-then-else structure. The IF formula requires three pieces of information. The first is a condition to be tested. In our example, the condition is H2>=70. The second piece of information tells how the value of the current cell is to be computed if the condition is true. In our case, this is the "P" which says the value of the current cell should become P if the condition is true. The third piece of information tells how to obtain the value if the condition is false. Copy the formula from I2 to the cells I3 through I16 to see the pass/fail grades as given by this formula. In the IF formula, we can give a complicated formula in the second or third position. In fact, we can give another IF formula if we wish. For example, if we wanted to give P+ for an average of 90 or above, the formula would be

"=IF(H2>=70,IF(H2>=90,"P+","P"),"F")"

Check that the following formula would also work:

"=IF(H2>=90,"P+",IF(H2>=70,"P","F"))".

Now let's proceed to assign the A-F letter grades. There are many ways to do this, and you are free to try your own method. One strategy is to assign A's to the 90 or above averages, then from the remainder assign B's to those above 80, etc. A formula for this would be

"=IF(H2>=90,"A",IF(H2>=80,"B",IF(H2>=70,"C",IF(H2>=60,"D","F"))))"

Enter a formula for cell I2 and copy it to cells I3-I16. The sheet should now look like Figure 18.5.

	A	B	C	D	E	F	G	H	I
1	**Name**	**Lab 1**	**Lab 2**	**Lab 3**	**Lab 4**	**Lab 5**	**Lab 6**	**Avg**	**Grade**
2	Miller, Bob	88	92	86	80	91	94	89	B
3	Bong, Chang	95	87	92	96	89	93	92	A
4	Wilson, Mary	84	60	82	78	80	70	76	C
5	Pavlovic, Martin	92	86	94	80	82	76	85	B
6	Carter, Louis	65	70	75	60	68	77	69	D
7	Sokol, Adrian	60	0	50	70	40	0	37	F
8	Duncan, Jim	95	98	94	60	88	92	88	B
9	Johnson, Carl	86	82	90	92	80	84	86	B
10	Artel, Lois	74	66	55	74	70	72	69	D
11	Taylor, Charles	86	82	90	85	78	80	84	B
12	Roberts, Victoria	98	88	85	84	92	96	91	A
13	Alou, Pedro	76	78	70	80	72	82	76	C
14	Adams, Ben	86	80	78	74	77	72	78	C
15	Beckley, John	66	50	52	54	64	68	59	F
16	Smith, Debbie	78	82	75	80	70	72	76	C
17									
18	**Lab Averages**	82	73	78	76	76	75	77	

Figure 18.5   Letter Grades Computed

To get the grades centered in the cells, select the cells you wish to center, and then click on the centering button on the button bar (Figure 18.6).

168 Laboratory Manual

Handwritten: ARRAY FORMULA: =SUM(IF(B12:B20="A",1,0))

Figure 18.6   Using the Centering Button

Exercise 18.6. Grade frequencies.

Next, suppose we want cells that hold the number of each letter grade we're currently assigning according to column I. Let's put headers for these cells in row 20, say headers of A in B20, B in C20, C in D20, D in E20 and F in F20. We'll store the number of A's in B21, B's in C21, etc. To compute the number of A's, for example, we'll make use of an *array formula*. An array formula takes an array of cells and computes a value for each cell. In our case, we'll use the IF function to look at the cells in the range I2 through I16. If the entry is "A", we'll have the IF compute a 1; otherwise, it will compute 0. Then we'll use the SUM function to add up these values. In this way it will add 1 for the cells with "A" and 0 for the other cells. The formula would look like "=SUM(IF(I2:I16="A",1,0))". However, when we enter an array formula in a cell, we indicate that we have used an array formula by holding down the Ctrl and Shift keys while pressing the Enter key. Go ahead and enter the formulas for the grade frequencies. The sheet should now appear as in Figure 18.7.

Handwritten:
= AVERAGE (B1:B2)
= ROUND(AVERAGE(B1:B2),0)
= IF(D1="D", "YES","NO")
= IF(A1="80",IF(A1=85, "A+", A), "F")
= SUM(IF (A1:A12="A",1,0))

	A	B	C	D	E	F	G	H	I
1	Name	Lab 1	Lab 2	Lab 3	Lab 4	Lab 5	Lab 6	Avg	Grade
2	Miller, Bob	88	92	86	80	91	94	89	B
3	Bong, Chang	95	87	92	96	89	93	92	A
4	Wilson, Mary	84	60	82	78	80	70	76	C
5	Pavlovic, Martin	92	86	94	80	82	76	85	B
6	Carter, Louis	65	70	75	60	68	77	69	D
7	Sokol, Adrian	60	0	50	70	40	0	37	F
8	Duncan, Jim	95	98	94	60	88	92	88	B
9	Johnson, Carl	86	82	90	92	80	84	86	B
10	Artel, Lois	74	66	55	74	70	72	69	D
11	Taylor, Charles	86	82	90	85	78	80	84	B
12	Roberts, Victoria	98	88	85	84	92	96	91	A
13	Alou, Pedro	76	78	70	80	72	82	76	C
14	Adams, Ben	86	80	78	74	77	72	78	C
15	Beckley, John	66	50	52	54	64	68	59	F
16	Smith, Debbie	78	82	75	80	70	72	76	C
17									
18	Lab Averages	82	73	78	76	76	75	77	
19									
20		A	B	C	D	F			
21		2	5	4	2	2			

Figure 18.7 Grade Frequencies Computed

Again, you could experiment with making a drastic change to one of the lab scores and watch the effects in the student's average, the student's grade, the lab average and the grade frequencies. Put the value back to the original before moving on to the next exercise.

Exercise 18.7. Chart of grade frequencies

Spreadsheet packages typically have extensive capabilities for making graphs of the data stored in the sheet. As with most features, there are various ways to get into the graphing or charting modes. In Excel, most straightforward charting tasks can be accomplished with the use of a tool called the ChartWizard. To explore its use, select the cells in the rectangle from B20 through F21 and then click on the ChartWizard button on the button bar (Figure 18.8). A dialog box like that in Figure 18.9 should appear. This screen

Figure 18.8 Choosing the Chart Wizard

allows you to choose the type of chart that you would like to use. We'll make a pie chart with the frequencies as the data and the headers as the section labels. Click on the **Pie** option and then on the first Chart sub-type.

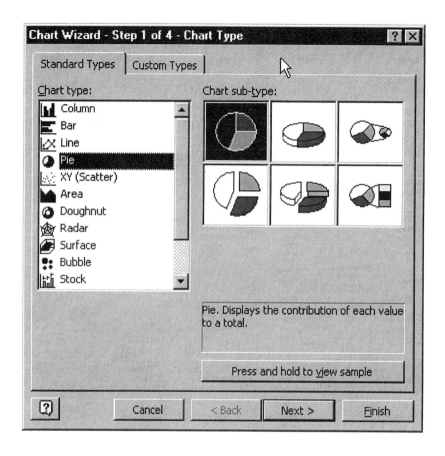

Figure 18.9 Selecting the chart type

Click on the **Next** button to move to the next dialog box (Figure 18.10). This second dialog box lets us specify whether the data series we wish to chart is a row or in a column. You should click the **Rows** button,

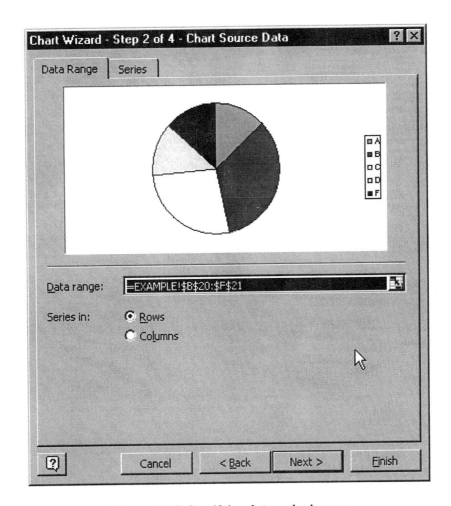

Figure 18.10 Specifying data series in rows

and then click on the **Next** button. This dialog box (Figure 18.11) allows us to include titles, legends and data labels. Under **Data labels** click on the **Show percent** button to have the data sections labeled with the corresponding percentages. Now click on the **Next** button to move to the dialog box of Figure 18.12. This dialog box allows us to have the chart as a separate sheet or to keep it with the Example spreadsheet we are working on - we want the latter. Now click on the **Finish** button to complete the work with the ChartWizard. The chart should now appear as in Figure 18.13. You can now use the cursor to resize and position the chart as you please.

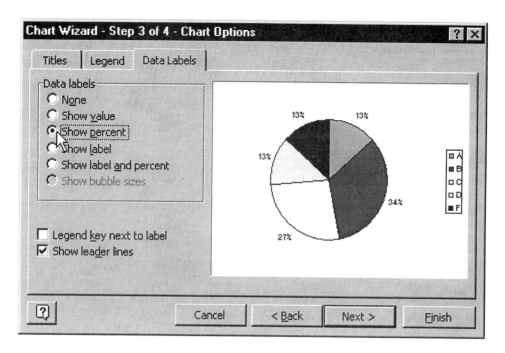

Figure 18.11 Choosing percentages as data labels

Figure 18.12 Keeping the chart with the spreadsheet

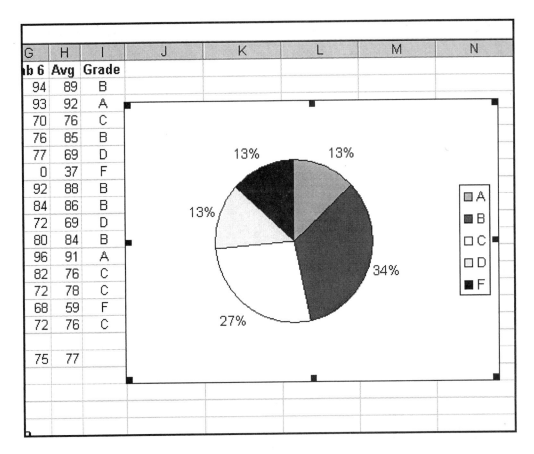

Figure 18.13 The Grade Distribution Chart

Exercise 18.8. Adjusting the grades

Suppose now that the grades seem a little too low. Let's experiment with a new formula. We could simply lower the numerical range for each letter grade, but instead, let's consider what would happen if we dropped the lowest lab grade for each student. In several cases, it seems that one bad day has made a substantial change in the overall grade. This is one advantage of spreadsheets over a traditional gradebook - its easy to perform "what if" experiments. Perhaps the easiest way to do the calculation would be to sum all of the lab grades and then subtract out the lowest grade. We would then divide the remaining sum by 5 to get the average. So, move to cell H2, and enter the formula

$$\text{"=ROUND((SUM(B2:G2)-MIN(B2:G2))/5,0)"}$$

Now copy the formula to cells H2 through H16. Note the changes in the averages, letter grades, grade distribution, and even in the chart! When you have finished, you should follow you instructor's directions for turning in your spreadsheet or having it checked at this point.

Lab Experience 19

Symbolic Computation
Curve Fitting

Objectives

In this lab session, you will make use of a symbolic computation package to experiment with fitting curves to sets of points as described in section 11.4 of the text. This lab experience is based on the Mathematica package that was covered in the text. If you are using a different package, your instructor should provide the necessary modifications. The main objective is to give you an introductory experience with this kind of tool. More and more, courses in science and mathematics make extensive use of such tools. These packages are quite extensive, providing many subpackages and even their own programming languages. We have chosen to focus on the topic of curve fitting to let you see how we might develop conjectures about the efficiency characteristics of an algorithm from test data. We assume that your instructor will show you how to access Mathematica on your computer system. You will not be writing programs, but rather working in an interactive mode where you simply type commands and see what happens. You are encouraged to try out the commands presented in the text.

Background

For purposes of this lab session, let's assume that we are trying to analyze a sort algorithm to determine its efficiency characteristics. Is it $\theta(n^2)$, $\theta(n \text{ Lg } n)$, or what? Suppose we time the algorithm with various sizes of test data and obtain a set of data points of the form (n, t) where n is the number of items being sorted, and t is the time it takes the algorithm to sort the items. One thing we can do is to plot the points and try to visually determine the nature of the relationship between n and t.

With curve fitting techniques, we can do better than this. Here we supply the symbolic computation package with the set of points and with a set of "ingredient" functions, and the package will determine a linear combination of the ingredient functions which best fits the set of points. By plotting this function along with the data points, we can get a good idea as to whether or not the ingredients are appropriate for the data points.

For example, if we suspect a quadratic relationship, then we're thinking that a relationship of the form

$$t = An^2 + Bn + C$$

might apply to the given algorithm. Here n^2, n and 1 (the multiplier of C) would be the ingredient functions. The symbolic computation package would determine the values for A, B and C which would best fit the given set of data points. By plotting the data points along with the function, we should be able to get a pretty good idea as to whether our suspicion of a quadratic relationship has merit. To investigate an n Lg(n) relationship, we might try n Lg(n), n and 1 as the ingredients (this is not the only possibility, however).

Suppose the set of data points is $\{(n_1,t_1),(n_2,t_2), ..., (n_k,t_k)\}$, and the proposed relationship is given by t=f(n). If this function gave a perfect fit, then we would have $t_1=f(n_1)$, $t_2=f(n_2)$, etc. Otherwise, $f(n_i)-t_i$ would give the error at the ith point. If we want the error to be positive, we could square it. The symbolic computation package provides what is called the *least squares best fit* curve. Here the coefficients for the ingredient functions are determined in such a way as to minimize the sum of the squares of the error terms.

One problem that we might encounter with the plan proposed above is that with a relatively small number of points, it is possible to get a pretty good fit for the given points even though the fit would not extend to points significantly outside the range of the sample points. Our modified plan, then, is to first fit the original sample. Then we will test this result to see how well it predicts the value for other points obtained from the algorithm, but with a significantly larger value of n. This corresponds closely to the lab work you did in Lab Experience 6 where we knew the efficiency characteristics and used them, together with sample results, to predict the time for larger values. If the fitting function is appropriate, it should also fit the new points fairly well.

Exercise 19.1. Defining the first set of points

You should now access the Mathematica package. Define the set of points for the next several exercises by typing in the following command exactly as given:

Points1 = {{50,2},{100,6},{200,13},{500,38},{1000,85},{2000,188}}

You should now see something like the following response from the package.

In[1]:=Points1 = {{50,2},{100,6},{200,13},{500,38},{1000,85},{2000,188}}

Out[1]={{50,2},{100,6},{200,13},{500,38},{1000,85},{2000,188}}

Let's assume that we have two other data points, {5000,527} and {10000,1139}, and that we want to see how well various fitting functions will predict these values. We will let Points2 be the total list of points. To obtain Points2 from Points1, type the following two commands.

Points2=Append[Points1,{5000,527}]

AppendTo[Points2,{10000,1139}]

Exercise 19.2 Fitting a quadratic to Points1

To find the quadratic, Q1, that best fits the set of data points, type the following command:

Q1[x_] = Fit[Points1, {1, x, x^2}, x]

Here, {1, x, x^2} is the set of ingredient functions, and x is the independent variable. It is important to type x underscore on the left and just x on the right (a peculiarity of the Mathematica syntax). Mathematica should now display the actual quadratic for Q1. Copy this quadratic onto the Worksheet.

Exercise 19.3 Predicting the additional points with Q1

We can now see the values that Q1 would predict for n=5000 (and n=10000) by simply typing Q1[5000] and Q1[10000]. Copy the numerical values for Q1[5000] and Q1[10000] onto the Worksheet.

Exercise 19.4 Plotting the Points1 and Q1

From the results of Exercise 19.3, we see that Q1 is not giving very accurate predictions. Just for practice, let's go ahead and plot the function Q1 and the data points. To see both Points2 and a graph of Q1 in the same figure, type the command

Show[Plot[Q1[x], {x,50,10000}], ListPlot[Points2]]

Here, we're asking Mathematica to show two things, the plot of Q1 and the plot of Points2. The notation {x,50,10000} indicates that we want to see the plot of Q1 with x values ranging from 50 through 10000. The result is shown in Figure 19.1.

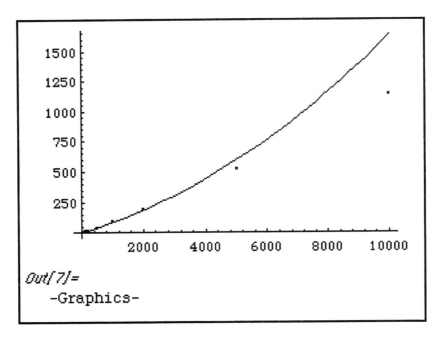

Figure 19.1 Plots of Q1 and Points1

Exercise 19.5   Fitting an n Lg(n) curve to Points1

To find the best fit, L1, with ingredients 1, x, and x Lg(x), type the command:

L1[x_] = Fit[Points1, {1, x, x Log[x]}, x]

Give the resulting expression for L1[x] on the Worksheet.

Exercise 19.6   Predicting the additional points with L1

Now see what L1 would predict for n=5000 (and n=10000) by simply typing N[L1[5000]] and N[L1[10000]]. Here we use the N to see the numerical value rather than a symbolic value using Log in the output expression. Copy the resulting values onto the Worksheet.

Exercise 19.7   Plotting Points2 and L1

To see both Points2 and a graph of L1 in the same figure, type the command

Show[Plot[L1[x], {x,50,10000}], ListPlot[Points2]]

The result should be as shown in Figure 19.2.

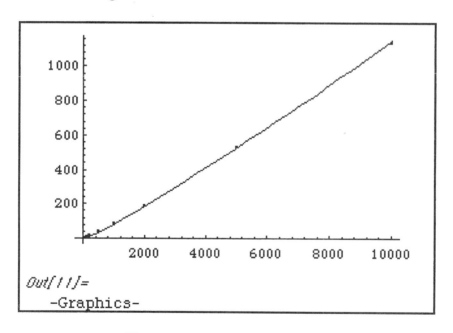

Out[11]=
   -Graphics-

Figure 19.2   Plots of Points2 and L1

From examining the plots of Figures 19.1 and 19.2, we would conjecture that the algorithm is θ(n Lg(n)) rather than θ(n²).

Exercise 19.8. Defining the second set of points

Define the set of points for the next several exercises by typing in the following command exactly as given:

Points3 = {{50,1},{100,1},{200,3},{500,8},{1000,21},{2000,68}}

Following the example of Exercise 19.1, give the commands to let Points4 be like Points3 only with the additional points {5000,365} and {10000,1382}.

Exercise 19.9 Fitting a quadratic to Points3

Find the quadratic, Q2, that best fits Points3. Give the expression for Q2 on the Worksheet.

Exercise 19.10 Predicting the additional points with Q2

Determine the values of Q2[5000] and Q2[10000] and see how well they compare with the data points. Give these values on the Worksheet.

Exercise 19.11 Plotting Points4 and Q2

Now plot Points4 and Q2 on the same graph.

Exercise 19.12 Fitting an n Lg(n) curve to Points3.

Find the best fit, L2, to Points3 using the ingredients 1, x, and x Log[x]. Give the expression for L2 on the Worksheet.

Exercise 19.13 Predicting the additional points with L2

Determine the values of L2[5000] and L2[10000] and see how well they compare with the data points. Give the values L2[5000] and L2[10000] on the Worksheet.

Exercise 19.14 Plotting Points4 and L2

Now plot Points2 and L2 on the same graph. From viewing the results of Exercise 19.11 and 19.14, what conjecture would you propose for the algorithm giving rise to Points4 (Worksheet)?

Exercise 19.15 The race is on

It appears that the algorithm, say A, for Points2 is $\theta(n \text{ Lg } n)$ while the algorithm, say B, producing Points4 is $\theta(n^2)$. For this reason, we tend to think the algorithm A is "better" than algorithm B. However, we note that B gives better times for lower values of n. Since L1 seems to give a good measure of the time for A and Q2 seems to model B, we can get an idea of the point at which A begins to excel by asking Mathematica to solve the equation L1[x] = Q2[x]. Do this now by typing the command

FindRoot[L1[x]==Q2[x],{x,50}]

Here we are indicating that the numerical solution package should begin the search at x=50. Give the resulting value on the Worksheet.

Worksheet
Lab Experience 19
Symbolic Computation
Curve Fitting

Name: _____

Course: _____

Exercise 19.2   Fitting a quadratic to Points1

   Q1[x] =

Exercise 19.3   Predicting the additional points with Q1

   Q1[5000] =

   Q1[10000] =

Exercise 19.5   Fitting an n Lg(n) curve to Points1

   L1[x] =

Exercise 19.6   Predicting the additional points with L1

   L1[5000] =

   L1[10000] =

Exercise 19.9   Fitting a quadratic to Points3

   Q2[x] =

Exercise 19.10   Predicting the additional points with Q2

Q2[5000] =

Q2[10000] =

Exercise 19.12   Fitting an n Lg(n) curve to Points3.

L2[x] =

Exercise 19.13   Predicting the additional points with L2

L2[5000] =

L2[10000] =

Exercise 19.14   Plotting Points4 and L2

Conjecture about L2:

Exercise 19.15   The race is on

Point at which L1[x] = Q2[x]:

Lab Experience 20

HTML and FTP Downloading

Objectives

In previous labs you have learned to use a web browser to navigate the World Wide Web. By completing the web exercises you have seen a number of interesting web pages related to various computer science topics. In Section 8.4 of the text you were introduced to HTML (HyperText Markup Language) which is the underlying formatting language for most web pages. Now in Chapter 12 of the text you have read about the history of the web, the algorithms and protocols that make such networking endeavors possible, and some of the social implications of the web. In this lab session you will practice using some of the most basic features of HTML to make your own web pages. This opens the door for you to become a contributor to the web enterprise rather than simply a user of the web. You will also learn how to use your web browser to perform simple file transfers from ftp servers.

Background

Creating web documents with HTML is somewhat analogous to writing programs in assembly language. Today there are many web editors available to simplify the process of writing web pages. In fact, the web browsers and most word processors include facilities for creating web pages. You might think of these web editors as the high level languages of web production. Just as programs written in high level languages such as C++, LISP, or PROLOG must be translated to machine or assembly language before they can be executed, documents written using web editors are converted to HTML before they are viewed as web pages. In this lab you will work directly with HTML. Just as learning a little about assembly language helps you understand what is going on inside the computer and helps you understand the features of a high level language, learning the basics of HTML is important for understanding the underlying process of web page formatting and design. Another practical reason for learning about HTML is you will often see some attractive feature that a web author has used on a page. Using your browser you will be able to look at the source of the page. However, the source will be the HTML file for the page. This is true even if a fancy web editor was used to create the document. So, to learn by example requires knowing about HTML. Once you have practiced the basic features of HTML, you may well want to learn to use a web editor. Most word processors and web browsers include tutorials that teach you how to use the special web editing features that they provide. The discussion that follows is based somewhat on "A Beginner's Guide to HTML" which was developed at the National Center for Supercomputer Applications and is present on many World Wide Web servers.

Recall from Section 8.4 of the text that much of the formatting of HTML is achieved with pairs of **tags** that enclose the text to which the formatting action applies. The beginning tag of a pair is usually of the form <action-symbol>, and the ending tag of the pair is of the form </action-symbol>. Here the action symbol is a special code indicating the manipulation that should be applied to the text enclosed between the pair of tags. For example, the symbol B indicates boldface. Thus <B> Lab Manual </B> in an HTML file causes the text "Lab Manual" to be displayed in boldface on the web page. Keep in mind that tag pairs can be nested within each other just as parentheses pairs can be nested in arithmetic expressions. For example, the HTML expression

<B> Just bold <I> Both bold and italic </I> Just bold </B> Plain

displays on the page as

Just bold *Both bold and italic* Just bold Plain

since the italic tag pair is included within the bold tag pair. Here is a list of basic tags together with their uses. Unless mentioned specifically, these occur in pairs. There are many books and online tutorials on HTML. There you will find more tags and HTML features.

HTML This tag indicates that the enclosed material is written in HTML. Therefore your entire HTML document should begin with <HTML> and end with </HTML>.

HEAD There are two major sections of an HTML document - the head and the body. This tag and its partner mark the beginning and end of the head section. This section does not contain material that will actually appear on the page itself. Primarily, it contains the title of the document.

TITLE This tag and its partner enclose the title of the page. This is placed within the head section of the document. The title does not appear on the page itself but does appear in the title bar of the window. Another important use of the title is that it appears in the bookmark list if the page has been saved by anyone as a bookmark.

BODY This pair of tags marks the beginning and end of the body section of the document. This section includes all of the text of the page together with the HTML tags for formatting the page and linking the page to other pages on the web. These four tags are actually enough to create a simple web page. As mentioned Section 8.4 of the text, a minimal HTML document would look like this:

```
<HTML>
<HEAD>
<TITLE> Title of your choice  </TITLE>
</HEAD>
<BODY>
        Text of your choice
</BODY>
</HTML>
```

If you created such a file with a text editor and named the file with a file name ending in .html, you should be able to open the file as a web page using your web browser.

H1   There are six levels of headings in HTML. These are numbered H1 through H6 with H1 being the largest and boldest. These are used to provide headings for divisions of your page. For example, you might use H1 for the main heading of your page and use H2 for section headings within the page. Some browsers may not distinguish six distinct levels.

P   This tag is used to mark the beginning of a new paragraph. HTML ignores line breaks and extra spaces between words in the text. Therefore the P tag is important to cause line separation between paragraphs. Optionally, you can use the P tag to specify how the paragraph should be aligned. For example, you can use <P ALIGN=CENTER> to center the paragraph on the page.

UL   HTML supports several types of lists such as unnumbered lists, numbered or ordered lists and definition lists. This tag indicates an unnumbered, bulleted list.

OL   This tag is used for ordered or numbered list. Note that lists can be nested with different list types being nested within each other.

LI   This tag indicates the beginning of a list item within a list. No closing tag is needed. You should now study carefully the HTML file shown in Figure 20.1. Be sure that you understand how the nested lists produce the page shown in Figure 20.2. Here we have two ordered lists nested as list items within the unnumbered list.

```
<HTML>
<HEAD>
<TITLE> Programming Languages </TITLE>
</HEAD>
<BODY>
<H1> Programming Languages in CS322 </H1>
<H2> An Outline of Languages </H2>
<UL>
<LI> Procedural Languages
<OL>
<LI> FORTRAN
<LI> COBOL
<LI> Pascal
<LI> C
<LI> Ada
</OL>
<LI> Object Oriented Languages
<OL>
<LI> C++
<LI> Java
<LI> Smalltalk
</OL>
</UL>
</BODY>
</HTML>
```

Figure 20.1 An HTML file with nested lists.

```
Programming Languages in CS322

An Outline of Languages

    • Procedural Languages
            1. FORTRAN
            2. COBOL
            3. Pascal
            4. C
            5. Ada
    • Object Oriented Languages
            1. C++
            2. Java
            3. Smalltalk
```

Figure 20.2 The web page produced from HTML code of Figure 20.1.

BR   This tag causes a line break to occur. While the P tag causes a blank line to appear between the paragraphs, the BR tag simply causes the following text to appear on the next line. Since regular line feeds in the text are ignored, this is an important feature for those situations where you want to make sure that the following text begins on a new line. The BR tag is used alone without an end tag.

HR   This horizontal rule tag also occurs without an end tag and causes a neat horizontal line to occur. This is often used to separate sections of a page.

B   As mentioned earlier, this tag pair is used to have text appear in boldface.

I   Again, this is used for putting text in Italics.

A   The anchor tag pair is used to create links - probably the most important feature in HTML. This topic is complicated because of the wide variety of types of objects that we might wish to access via links. The possibilities include other pages within the same directory as the current page, other pages on the same web server but in another directory, specific locations within the current page or other pages, pages stored on other World Wide Web servers, images (sound, video, etc.) at any of these locations, files to be downloaded from ftp servers which allow public access for such purposes, and telnet services allowing the use of computational resources on another computer. Here we discuss how to link to pages in the same directory, to pages on other servers using URLs, to other locations within the current page, and to objects on public ftp servers. Later in this section, we discuss linking to images and to public ftp servers.

In addition to the code A, the beginning tag contains the target address for the link. The form for this tag is <A HREF="target-address">. If we are linking to another file in the same directory, then the target address is simply the file name. Note that filenames of HTML files should always end in .html. To link to files in other directories, you must use the pathname to the file. To link to pages on other servers, you simply use the URL as the target address in the tag. As you know, URLs to web pages begin with *http*. This indicates that we are linking to a file on a World Wide Web server. There are specifications other than *http* that allow linking to objects other than web pages. For example, ftp indicates that we are linking to an ftp server that allows public access, and *telnet* indicates a link to a server providing computational services. We shall discuss the ftp option more fully a little later in this section.

The end tag is simply </A> as you would expect. Between the two tags is the text that should appear highlighted and which is clicked to execute the link. For example, if you wanted a link from your page to the web exercises index page for this lab manual, you could put in the HTML expression

<A HREF=http://www.wlu.edu/~whaleyt/invitation/lab.html> Web Exercises </A>

which would use "Web Exercises" as a link to activate the web exercise page.

With long documents it is often convenient to have links to various sections within the document. For example, if the document is divided into chapters, you might like to have a table of contents at the beginning with links to the various chapters. To do this requires not only the links to go to the various chapters, but also a new type of anchor naming locations within the document to which we can link. The form for this new type of anchor is

<A NAME="location-name"> Location-title </A>.

Here the location name is a name that will be used in the anchors that link to this spot, and the location title will appear at the top of the screen when such a link is activated. For example, if we wish to allow links to Chapter 2 on tree searching algorithms, we could provide a name anchor of the form

<A NAME="Ch2"> Chapter 2 - Tree Searching Algorithms </A>.

Since we want the chapter title to serve as a heading, we would probably include the entire anchor within a heading tag pair, say like

<H2> <A NAME="Ch2"> Chapter 2 - Tree Searching Algorithms </A> </H2>.

Now to provide a link to such a named location, the anchor is of the form

<A HREF="#location-name"> Link-text </A>

where location-name is the named location to which we are linking, and Link-text is the text for the highlighted link used to activate the transfer. So, in the table of contents we might have links of the form

<A HREF="#Ch2"> Chapter 2 </A>

or

<A HREF="#Ch2"> Tree Searching Algorithms </A>

or

<A HREF="#Ch2"> Chapter 2 - Tree Searching Algorithms </A>,

etc.

IMG This tag occurs without a partner and is used for displaying images on a page. As discussed in the text, images are stored as special files with information such as color for each pixel of the image. There are several formats that are widely used for storing such images. Two of the most common formats are GIF and JPEG, and files in these formats are named with endings *.gif* and *.jpeg*, respectively. The web browsers are usually capable of displaying images that are stored in these formats. The form of the anchor is

<IMG SRC=image-location>

where the image location is the file name of the image on the computer where the page is stored or the URL for the image file on another computer. For example, if you have a picture of yourself stored in the file *me.gif*, then you can have it displayed on your page using the anchor

<IMG SRC=me.gif>.

The IMG tag also allows an optional ALIGN clause following the filename. This has to do with how the image is aligned with the text. For example,

<IMG SRC=me.gif ALIGN=CENTER>

will place the image at the left with one line of text to the right of the image and centered vertically with the picture. You can also use TOP rather than CENTER. This puts one line to the right and at the top of the picture. The default is to have the one line of text to the right of the bottom line of the picture. To have a picture appear by itself without text to the right, put the IMG tag in a paragraph by itself. You can then use ALIGN with the paragraph tag to justify the image as you please. You can also link to an image using an anchor. For example, if you have a large picture of yourself that you do not want to appear on your page, you might use a link such as the following

<A HREF="me.gif"> A picture of me </A>.

If someone clicks on the words "A picture of me", the browser should display your picture.

To create an HTML file, you can use any text editor or word processor. Once you have created an HTML file on your local computer, you can view the resulting page with your web browser. To do this, take the **Open file in browser** option under the **File** menu and then select the HTML file that you have created. If you need to make changes, you can edit the file in another window, save the file, and then use the **Reload** button of the browser to view the new version of your page. In order to have your page available for other users of the web, your file HTML file must be stored on a web server. Most colleges and universities have web servers, but you will need to check with the local experts for the details for doing this. Many businesses have their own web servers or else pay for space on web servers of companies who specialize in providing internet services for their customers.

As with web servers, many institutions provide ftp servers. These servers usually have many directories each storing many related files. These files may be textual documents, graphics, or pieces of special purpose software that can be transferred from the server to the user's local computer - this is called *downloading*. In order to download a file from an ftp server, you must be able to log onto the server machine. While many servers restrict access to authorized users, others allow *anonymous* logins. In this case the user name "anonymous" with any password - often your email address is requested as a password - yields access to the server. While there are many excellent programs specifically for managing ftp transfers, the standard web browsers can also be used for downloading files from ftp servers that allow anonymous logins. To use your browser for this purpose, simply use the ftp prefix in the URL rather than the http prefix. This type of URL can be used in the location field or in the anchor of a link. Exactly what the browser does with the file depends on the type of file accessed. If it is reasonable, the browser will display the text or image; otherwise, it may simply ask if you would like to save the file on your computer (download). In the former case, you can download the file by selecting the **Save** option under the **File** menu.

Exercise 20.1.   Viewing HTML code

In this exercise you will view the HTML code for the index page for the web exercises that you have used in other labs. Start up your browser and go to the index page http://wlu.edu/~invite. Now to view the HTML code for this page, choose **Document source** under the **View** menu. This should display the HTML source in another window. By comparing the source together with the page displayed, answer the following questions on the Worksheet page for this lab.

1. Give the title of the page.
2. Describe one use of lists on the page.
3. Describe one use of a link on the page.
4. Describe one tag used on the page that was not described in our discussion in the Background section of this lab.

Exercise 20.2.   Making your own page

For this exercise you will use a text editor or word processor to create an HTML file containing information about yourself. Your page should be divided into the following sections:

1. Brief family history.

2. Brief educational history. Include a list of schools you have attended. *edu.htm*
3. Current academic situation. Include information about your major, your current school (with a link to school's home page), and a list of courses your are taking.
4. Non-academic interests. Include information about hobbies, favorite musical groups, etc. *int.htm*

You should have a table of contents at the beginning with links to the various sections. Separate the sections with horizontal lines. To view your page, run your web browser and select the **Open file in browser** option under the **File** menu and then select the HTML file that you have created. When you have the page the way you want it, click on the **Print** button of the browser to print a copy of the page to turn in. To get a copy of the HTML code to turn in, use the **Print** option under the **File** menu of your text editor or word processor.

Exercise 20.3.   Downloading with the browser

In this exercise, you will simply download a text file from an ftp server. To do this type the URL

ftp://wlu.edu/pub/invite/lab20.txt

into the location field of your browser. The browser will probably display the short text file. You should then select the **Save** option under the **File** menu to bring the file from the server to your computer.

Worksheet
Lab Experience 20
HTML and FTP Downloading

Name: _____

Course: _____

Exercise 20.1. Viewing HTML code

Page title: _____

Use of lists:

Use of a link:

New use of a tag:

Lab Experience 21

Neural Networks

Objectives

This lab introduces you to the use of neural networks. We provide a neural net application that recognizes characters. You will tell the network which characters to learn, provide it with training data, and test the network's recognition capability.

Background

A neural network consists of a set of input nodes, a set of output nodes, and one or more hidden layers of nodes that connect the input nodes to the output nodes. Input and output nodes can represent patterns, such as characters or images of faces, to be recognized by the network. For example, in the case of characters, pieces of a character in a visual field can map to individual input nodes in the network. To acquire knowledge of this pattern, the user trains the net by giving it the pattern as a desired output node and asking the net to train itself. The net trains itself by placing this pattern on its input nodes and running perhaps several iterations until the connections from input nodes to the output node reach a certain value. After the net has been trained to recognize a given pattern, the user can present it with this pattern or a similar one as a trial input and ask the net to solve for the input pattern. If the input pattern is similar enough to one of the patterns represented in the net's set of output nodes, the net informs the user that it recognizes the input as the pattern represented by that node; otherwise, the net does not recognize the input pattern.

The neural net simulator provides you with the following features:

1. A built-in network.
2. The ability to draw new output nodes (patterns to be recognized).
3. The ability to train the net to recognize these patterns.
4. The ability to give the net trial patterns as inputs and attempt to solve for them.

Open the neural net lab by selecting **Neural Network** from the main menu. You should see the window in Figure 21.1.

Figure 21.1 The Neural Net Window

The neural net window consists of the following panes:

1. **Input/Output Sets** (upper left pane). Here you can edit patterns to be added as output nodes to the net. You can transfer these patterns to and from files or from the **Visual Field** (see below).
2. **Visual Field** (upper middle pane). Here you can edit patterns to be presented as trial inputs to the net. You can transfer these patterns to and from files or from the **Input/Output Sets**.
3. **Results** (upper right pane). The results of training or solving are displayed here.
4. **The Neural Net** (lower pane). Here is a visual representation of the neural net. The input nodes are at the bottom and the output nodes are at the top.

The three menus allow you to manage the net, the output nodes, and the visual field.

Exercise 21.1 Training the network to recognize the letter A

In this exercise, you will train the network to recognize the letter A. A training session consists of the entering the character to be learned and training the net. To get started, perform the following steps:

1. Select the **Add Output Node** button.

2. Enter the letter A in the prompter, select the radio button **Visual Field From File**, and click **OK** (Figure 21.2).

3. Select the file Character'A'.vfl and click **OK**.

Figure 21.2 Adding an output node for the letter A

Then select **Train**. Your application window should look like the one in Figure 21.3.

Figure 21.3 Training a neural network for the letter A

Note that the net now has a single output node. Each connection from this node to the net represents a black square in the pattern for the letter A. The net also took 24 iterations to learn this letter.

Exercise 21.2 Solving for a test character

Let's test the recognition capability of the network trained in the previous exercise. There three ways to create a sample pattern for input:

1. Click the button Copy Field from Selected I/O Set.
2. Open a visual field pattern from a file (Visual Field Menu).
3. Draw the pattern by hand (clicking the squares in the visual field pane).

Step 1 is the easiest so do that now. Then click the **Solve** button. The window should look like the one in Figure 21.4.

Figure 21.4 Solving for the letter A

The window now has several changes:

1. The input pattern appears in the visual field pane.
2. The input nodes corresponding to the black squares in this pattern are highlighted in the net.

3. The results of recognizing the input pattern are displayed in the results pane.

Exercise 21.3 Editing a test character

Human beings are able to recognize letters and other objects even though they might only be approximations of some ideal types. To test the neural net's recognition capability, we can remove pieces of the letter A and observe the outputs. Remove the top two dots on the bitmap by right-clicking the mouse on them. Then select **Solve** from the **Neural Net Commands** menu. Then try removing one dot at a time from the next row and solving each time. Describe what the character looks like to you.

Exercise 21.4 Training for more than one character

The real power of a neural network lies in its ability to distinguish several different objects. To see how this is so, let's train a net to recognize the letters A, B, and O. To clear the current network, select **New** from the **Net** menu. Then, select **Add Output Node** three times to enter the three letters from their respective files. When you select **Train**, the network learns the three characters concurrently. After training, your window should look like the one in Figure 21.5.

Figure 21.5 A neural net after entering three characters

Try solving for each input letter after placing each letter in the visual field pane. Now delete the top two rows of squares in the visual field's letter A and solve. Explain the results.

Exercise 21.5. How much can the net handle?

Add a character at a time to the I/O set for the net from Exercise 21.4 and train after each one is entered. You might have to click the **Train** button several times before the net is trained for a given character. Then explain the results.

Worksheet
Lab Experience 21
Neural Networks

Name: _____

Course: _____

Exercise 21.2 Solving for a test character

Exercise 21.3 Editing a test character

Exercise 21.4 Training for more than one character

Exercise 21.5. How much can the net handle?